THE ULTIMATE AUDITION BOOK FOR TEENS:

111 One-Minute Monologues

A Smith and Kraus Book
Published by Smith and Kraus, Inc.
177 Lyme Road, Hanover, NH 03755
www.SmithandKraus.com

First Edition: June 2000
9 8 7 6 5 4 3 2

Library of Congress Cataloging-in-Publication Data

Milstein, Janet B.
The ultimate audition book for teens : 111 one-minute monologues / by Janet B. Milstein.-- 1st ed.
p. cm. -- (Young actors series)
Summary: A collection of 111 original monologues, all about one minute long, to be used by male and female teenage actors in auditions.
ISBN-10: 1-57525-236-8   ISBN-13: 978-1-57525-236-0
1. Monologues. 2. Acting. 3. Auditions. [1. Monologues.
2. Acting--Auditions.] I. Title. II. Young actor series.
PN2080 .M47 2000
812'.6--dc21
00-035864

THE ULTIMATE AUDITION BOOK FOR TEENS:

111 One-Minute Monologues

By
Janet B. Milstein

YOUNG ACTORS SERIES

A Smith and Kraus Book

SPECIAL THANKS

I would like to express my deepest gratitude to Barbara Lhota. I cannot thank her enough for all of her time, feedback, patience, and support as I endlessly subjected her to one monologue after the other. She is an extraordinary person, a gifted writer, and a true friend.

I would also like to thank Karen Milstein for editing the non-monologue text in this book. She is a fabulous writer and editor, and I am truly honored and lucky to have her as my sister.

In addition, I am extremely grateful to Maureen Aitken for kindly offering me her guidance, advice, knowledge, and time at the beginning stages of my efforts. She is a remarkably talented writer and a wonderful person.

ACKNOWLEDGMENTS

I would like to thank the following people for their generous work on the monologues in this book, and others for their inspiration and support:

Maureen Aitken
Jamie Allain
Robert "Bobby" Allen
Jason Amato
Mary Elisabeth Armstrong
Brendan Arnold
Alexandra Bean
James Bezy
Allie Bianchi
Melanie Braxton
Carla Bruni
Adam Budz
Lauren Carnevale
Edson Castillo
Crystal Celestaine
Marissa Cerar
Justin Cholewa
Philip Cole
Angelique Cooper
Ellen Crabill
Yolanda Craig
Chris Cullen
Martin Czerep
Heather Dannewitz
Erin Davidson-Mary
Eric Davis
Mark Davis
Anthony DiGiorgio
Jenni Dunn
Joseph Durkin

Eleni Filippi
Brittani Franklin
Lacey Free
Jennifer Gifford
Cosima Mina Greco
Tracy Gromek
Michael Harrah
Taylor Harris
Patricia Heath
Allison Hillary
Jane Hoffman
Patrick Johnson
Barbara Kanady
Jenna Klym
Millie Larson
Christy LaVigne
Jessica Lewis
John Lewis III
Stephanie Magoon
Alice Mayo
John Miller
Amethyst Milstein
Donald Milstein
Freda Milstein
Karen Milstein
Karen "Kovy" Milstein
Kathryn Milstein
Joshua Milstein
Melissa Milstein
Natalie "Novy" Milstein

Peggy "Darla D" Milstein
Jessel Monteverde
George Moskal
Marisa Nasti
Charlotte Noordzy
Donna & Drew Peel
Danielle Plesh
LaNeda Pitts
Dianna Poulos
Victor Pratt
Amber Rabe
Brandon Ramsey
Alma Ruiz
Jeremy Sklar
Diana Skrypek
Sharon Smyers
Ricky Staub
Brenda Stock
Kimberly Tabor
Coretha Timko
Angela Ventrella
Greg Vojtanek
Chas Vrba
Kevin Walsh
Stephanie Welander
Alison Wilbur
Heather Winter
Matt Wisner
Jennifer Yale

Contents

INTRODUCTION

A s an actor and acting teacher, I am all too familiar with the difficult task of finding a good monologue. After listening to my peers and students voice the same frustrations, I decided to try writing monologues specifically for them. Remarkably, they loved the pieces, and I was grateful that they had helped me discover a dormant talent. Then came the second request. "I only have a minute. Can you cut this down?" It's true that most audition slots have shortened from the standard two-minute to one-minute intervals. How could I refuse?

About the same time I began training actors to participate in the International Modeling and Talent Association (IMTA) competitions. The conventions are huge, the competition is steep, and the agents, casting directors, and personal managers come from all over the world to scout for new talent. Actors would be asked to perform comedic and dramatic monologues. The time allotted? You guessed it...one minute. Unfortunately, when these actors showed me their selected monologues, it seemed that every piece was overdone, not in their casting range, requiring dialects, inactive, or, most importantly, not showcasing their potential. The teenagers were having an especially hard time finding good pieces because there are so few monologues from plays for actors in their age range. Furthermore, the original pieces they found usually sounded like speeches to no one in particular and presented the actors as cranky, whiny, rude, or (like, ya know, like, ya know) dumb. What they needed were powerful, direct, one-minute monologues in language and situations they could relate to without being stereotyped as obnoxious. I picked up a pen and a tiny notebook and dove in. The result is this book.

Many of the pieces have now been performed at the IMTA conventions by actors I have coached. Some have won awards. Other monologues have been worked and revised but never performed in competition. Therefore, if an award is not noted, it does not mean a piece is less effective than those that won awards.

What you will find in the pages to follow is a multitude of monologues that are new to the public, but have been put to the test. They are packed with emotional depth, hilarious experiences, honesty, pain, and charm, in a variety of voices that you can relate to. The monologues have direct, active openings that immediately connect the actor to the "invisible other." No dialects or accents are required. The majority of the pieces are one minute in length; I have included a few that are slightly shorter or longer. Most importantly, the pieces in this book are written in *real* language and *real* situations, and they are *really* fun to work on.

I have given titles to the monologues in this book. DO NOT LOOK FOR PLAYS WITH THESE TITLES BECAUSE THEY DO NOT EXIST. I titled the pieces simply for convenience when auditioning since an actor is often asked, "So, what will you be doing for us today?" Think of the monologues as titled solo pieces.

My hope is that you will find not one but several monologues within these pages to use for virtually all of your audition needs. And when it is time to expand your repertoire, you will come back to this book to choose more. Good hunting, best wishes, have fun, and break a leg!

Janet B. Milstein

HOW TO USE THIS BOOK

I have tried to make this book as easy to use as possible, so I divided it into a few distinct categories. First, I have separated Female, Male, and Male or Female monologues. Each of these categories is then broken down into comedic and dramatic monologues, so you can quickly find what you need.

You will notice that there are no age ranges indicated for the monologues in this book. I chose to leave them open-ended since teenagers mature at a varied pace and often look much older or younger than their actual age. However, to make searching easier, I have arranged the monologues in each category from youngest to oldest. But please note that some of the pieces can be done by a wider span of ages than others (one in particular was a hit when performed by an eighteen year old and a forty year old). Generally, your best bet is to look in the front of each section if you are thirteen or fourteen, the middle if you are mid-teens, and the middle to back pages if you are eighteen or older. Also consider your casting range, the nature of the material, and the audition situation. For example, a particular monologue that refers to college or driving would not seem realistic if performed by a fourteen year old. Use your best judgment.

I have included a few monologues in which the characters seem older than nineteen. They may come in handy when auditioning for school or community theatre, where young actors are often cast in older roles. These pieces will also present an exciting challenge in acting classes.

Lastly, you will see *(Beat)* in many of the monologues. A beat is a pause and is usually written to indicate that the other person is speaking. Since the lines of the other person are not included, it is your job to figure out exactly what he/she said to you. Choose specific dialogue that will best fuel you to respond. Be sure to look at the lines surrounding the beats. Examine the character's response for clues to guide you, so that the piece remains logical and coherent. Occasionally, the beat is used simply because the character has paused. In either case, it is up to the actor to make sure that the beats happen for a reason that is understandable, believable, and full of life.

FEMALE MONOLOGUES

COMEDIC

Small Talk

COMEDIC

Angie is a short girl with a big crush on Danny, a bas-
ketball player at school. She decided to go watch his
game in the hope that he'd ask her out. After the
game, and totally humiliated, she goes to her friend
Trisha's house.

Angie: Oh my God! Trisha, I'm so embarrassed! I went to Danny's basketball game today. I thought if he saw me there, he'd know how much I like him and he'd ask me out. He was definitely the cutest one on the team. Well, they won, so I ran to congratulate him. But all the guys on the team were crowding around and he didn't see me. So finally, I whistled real loud, and everyone stopped and looked down at me. I turned bright red! But Danny smiled, picked me up and twirled me around in a big hug! I was so excited!! Then one of the guys goes, "Hi there. You must be Danny's little sister." I thought I would die! I'm only two years younger than him — so what if I'm two feet shorter. Then this tall, blonde girl walked up to Danny and kissed him! Kissed him!! She wouldn't even be so tall if you didn't count her hair. I wanted to kick her, but I ran out instead. From now on, I'm going to watch the boys' Gymnastics Team. At least I could kiss one of them if I stood on my toes.

Award winner: Comedy Monologue Competition, International Modeling & Talent Association, Los Angeles 1999 Convention.

The Horrors of Holidays

COMEDIC

It is the day after Thanksgiving. Kara's friend asks her how her holiday was.

Kara: How was it? It was awful! I hate Thanksgiving. It's like one of those holidays designed to make people miserable. My brother wouldn't shut up about all this dumb football stuff. And my little sister started crying cause she wanted pizza. Pizza! Actually, I can't blame her. I mean, who invented the Jell-O mold anyway? It would be okay if it was just cranberry. But no, it's like this law that you have to put all kinds of disgusting fruit bits in it. Meanwhile, my aunt kept asking, "Soooo, do you have a boyfriend yet?" Like I'd tell her, even if I did. And my mom was running around, refusing to sit and eat. I think she must have always dreamed of being a waitress. Then my grandma announces she's suffering from gas. Who's she kidding? We were the ones suffering! Everyone pigged out and then lied around watching TV and feeling sick. So I figure, the reason we're giving thanks is that we only have to do this once a year!

Award winner: Comedy Monologue Competition, International Modeling & Talent Association, Los Angeles 2000 Convention.

A License to Date

COMEDIC

Jordan has asked April to go out with him to the movies. She is so excited. The only problem is that they need a ride. Here, she tries desperately to get her sister to agree to drive them.

April: Guess what?! Jordan asked me out! *(She squeals.)* I'm so psyched! We're gonna go to the movies tomorrow. There's just one thing. His brother can't drive us cause he has a date. So, I was wondering… *(Beat.)* Oh, c'mon Linda! I've been waiting for Jordan to ask me out for like my whole life. *(Beat.)* Okay, so three weeks — but it feels like my whole life! All we need is a ride. *(She lifts her hands like paws and pants like a dog. Beat.)* Oh, I already did. Mom can't take us cause she has her Pottery & Emotions class. Please? I'll do your chores tomorrow? *(Beat.)* All week?! What do I look like, Cinderella? Then I guess that makes you my ugly step-sister. Kidding — I'm kidding! Okay, I'll do it. But promise me you won't tell Jordan how much I like him. *(Beat.)* Well, if you do, I'll tell Mom you broke her Happiness frog.

The Perfect Guy

COMEDIC

Christine is at a dance, determined to meet the boy of her dreams. Suddenly, she is approached by a less-than-perfect guy.

Christine: I'm sorry but that seat is taken. I'm saving it for someone. He's the cutest, funniest, richest, coolest guy in the world and he's totally in love with me. *(Beat.)* No, it's not my boyfriend. You see, I don't know him yet. That's why I'm here at this dance. To meet him. To find him. Get it? *(Beat.)* How do I know it's not you? Well…I just know. Trust me. It's a girl thing. No offense, but I'm talking about my ultimate dream guy here. He has to have all of these really important, specific qualities. *(Beat.)* You have your own car? Wanna sit down and talk?

Dancing On Eggshells

COMEDIC

Alicia has been getting ready for the big dance. Earlier, her friend suggested washing her hair with eggs so it would be extra healthy and shiny. Her friend shows up, ready to go to the dance. Alicia is clearly upset, and her hair is sticking out all over the place.

Alicia: What's wrong? You're what's wrong! I can't go to the dance now. Look at my hair! You and your big ideas! "Put eggs in your hair. It'll make it all shiny and smooth." Right. I went to wash them out and they fried on my hair! *(Beat.)* It's not funny! You never told me I had to rinse with *cold* water! I tried scrubbing it out and it turned into scrambled eggs, stuck in clumps all over my head! It took two hours to get most of it out, and I still smell like an omelet. What am I supposed to do — wear toast for earrings and make it a theme?! Everything's ruined. There's no way I'm going to the dance with my hair sticking out like this. *(Beat.)* Okay, okay. Fine. Try to put it up. Go ahead. Make me a big, old sticky bun.

Award winner: Comedy Monologue Competition, International Modeling & Talent Association, New York 1999 & Los Angeles 2000 Conventions.

Barking Up Dates

COMEDIC

Sheri has a big crush on a guy from school. She went to a party where she knew she'd see him. It's the next day, and her friend is dying to know what happened.

Sheri: You should have seen me. It was great! As soon as I got to the party, I walked over and started talking to him. And I'm being real sweet and kinda shy, but still flirty at the same time, ya know? Well, I notice he keeps staring at my dress. Suddenly, I got all paranoid that the buttons had popped off and my bra was hanging out or something. So I fake a sneeze and peek down, and thank God, everything's where it should be. But he keeps on looking at it. So I say, "You like my dress, huh?" And he says, "It reminds me of my grandmother's tablecloth." I almost died! And it gets worse. Right then Kelly Johnson struts by and he winks at her and makes a motion like "call me." I lost it. I totally went off on him. I said, "You are rude and pathetic and it's no wonder you don't have a girlfriend! I wouldn't go out with you if you were the last breathing soul on earth!" And ya know what? It worked! We have a date Friday night!

Irresistible

A friend has just asked for advice on how to get a guy to fall for her. More experienced, Samantha eagerly shares her secrets.

Samantha: It's not very difficult. If you really want a guy to find you irresistible, here's what ya gotta do. First of all, always send him the signal that you're interested. Guys are so afraid of rejection, you gotta help build their confidence. Whenever you see him walking by, give him the look. *(Beat.)* Yeah, the look that says, "I want you." It's all in the eyes. Like this. *(She demonstrates.)* Unless he's blind, there's no way he's gonna miss that message. Next, you have to get the walk down. Sexy, like you know you're the bomb. Watch, it's like the motion of the ocean. C'mon, try it. Like the motion of the ocean. Good! And here's a special secret. When you talk to him, stare at his mouth a lot. Go on, pretend I'm him. *(Beat.)* Don't stare like I've got food stuck in my teeth! Stare at it like you want him to kiss you. You'll drive him crazy, trust me. So who's this cute guy you're after? *(Beat.)* Brandon?! Act like that around him, and I'll kill you!

Award winner: Comedy Monologue Competition, International Modeling & Talent Association, Los Angeles 2000 Convention.

Crawling to Paradise

COMEDIC

*Tracy has had a major crush on Robby for "a long time."
Tracy's best friend has just announced that Robby asked
her to the dance.*

Tracy: Whoa. Hold it. Stop right there. I know you didn't say
what I thought you just said. Robby asked you to the dance?
Robby? As in *my* Robby? As in, Robby who I've been in love
with since I could crawl? How can you do this to me? You're
supposed to be my best friend! You know I have plans to marry
him. *(Beat.)* So what if he doesn't even notice I'm alive — that's
not the point. The point is you back-stabbed me. You are unbelievable! You can't even — what? David wants to go with me?
David, as in, tall, blue-eyed, major babe David? Get out! Really?
How cool! We can double date! Oh my God, can you imag-
ine?! *(Beat.)* Of course I'm not mad at you. You're my best
friend! You and Robby are meant to be. Really, you are.
Besides, I've been in love with David since I could crawl.

Award winner: Comedy Monologue Competition, International Modeling &
Talent Association, Los Angeles 1999 & 2000 Conventions.

The Gravity of Graduating

Cindy's friend is upset because she spilled Hawaiian Punch on her dress at school. Cindy is not very sympathetic because her day was even more disastrous.

Cindy: That is nothing. My Physics exam was today. I had my alarm and the coffee pot set to go off at five. I had to cram. But when I woke up, it was seven o'clock! You should have seen me. I was brushing my teeth with one hand, putting on mascara with the other, and reading my Physics book with my free eye. I ran out the door with only one shoe on. I'm hobbling to school, eating my Poptart, memorizing, "Power equals Energy over Time, Power equals Energy over Time." My energy is way up, I'm on time, I have the power to do this! I plop down in the chair. I look down and the test booklet says, "The U.S. Constitution!" I studied for the wrong test! The wrong test! So I'm sorry you spilled Hawaiian Punch on your dress, but I'm about to fail the 11th grade!

There's Gotta Be a Better Way

COMEDIC

Faith works at McDonald's. She is having the day from hell. To make matters worse, she has been pestered twice by the same customer. When the customer complains for the third time, Faith loses it.

Faith: Ma'am, I replaced the first burger free cause it "didn't taste right" to you. And the second burger cause you said it wasn't cooked enough. Now you're telling me that this burger is burnt?! You have got to be kidding me. Where do you think you are? This is McDonald's! We ain't serving no sirloin steak! $5.25 an hour and I gotta put up with the likes of you. I'll tell you what. Why don't you come back here, take my greasy apron and my stupid, ugly hat, and stand back here in 128 degree temperature and cook your own burger till you're satisfied. Oh, and hey, don't forget you gotta smile nice for all the customers while you're sweating to death and the French Fry boys are whispering perverted jokes!! No? Doesn't sound like a good old time to you? Well then, I highly suggest you take that burger back to your little table, eat it, and think about how lucky you are that I didn't smush an apple pie in your face. Have I made myself clear? Thank you. Have a nice day.

Award winner: Comedy Monologue Competition, International Modeling & Talent Association, New York 1998, Los Angeles 1999, New York 1999, & Los Angeles 2000 Conventions.

Baby Mine

COMEDIC

*Monica recently spent her college money on an opera-
tion to have her ears pinned back. Her older brother (or
good friend.), Joey, is upset with her and can't understand why she'd do something so stupid. Here, Monica
tries to justify what she's done.*

Monica: Okay. Remember Dumbo? Cute little elephant, sweet
as can be, right? HUGE EARS! And what did they call him?
Dumbo! *(Beat.)* I know he flew at the end and became a star,
but that's just the Disney-happy-ending-thing. Big ears are not
attractive, Joey. Think about it. When was the last time you
thought, "Man, I'd love to date a girl with nice legs, and ears
that stick out to Timbuktu?!" Admit it — you never have. *No
one* has — unless they've got some weird ear fetish or something. So I got my ears pinned back. Big deal. I know that
money was supposed to be for college, but think how much I'll
learn, since now, I can hear people talking for miles behind me!

Award winner: Comedy Monologue Competition, International Modeling &
Talent Association, New York 1998 Convention.

Psyched Out

COMEDIC

Kama's boyfriend has just told her that he wants to break up. Kama uses her psychology to try to change his mind.

Kama: No, you're wrong. You don't really want to break up with me, you just *think* you do. Trust me. I've been psychologically in tune since birth. What's really going on is that somewhere deep inside of you, you feel you're unworthy of being loved. I bet that has to do with your mother. Anyway, when someone like me gets close to you, cares about you, it pushes that button. You think I'm going to hurt you and your impulse is to run away. But what you really want is to scream, "I want you to love me for who I am! Accept me with all of my faults and insecurities!" That's your problem. You're afraid of rejection. *(Beat.)* Hey, wait! Where are you going?

Award winner: Comedy Monologue Competition, International Modeling & Talent Association, Los Angeles 1999 Convention.

Daylight Savings

COMEDIC

Gillian hasn't had any luck finding a job. Her friend puts in a good word, and her boss agrees to hire Gillian. Gillian has just found out the good news.

Gillian: You rock! You are the coolest! No, you are beyond cool. You are like mucho, excellent, get-down-and-kiss-your-boots cool. I can't believe you got me the job! I can't believe it! You are so amazing. Man! So when do I start? *(Beat.)* Tomorrow? Yes, yes, kickin'! You, I love. What time do I have to be there? *(Beat.)* 7:30? Like 7:30 A.M.? Like, in the morning 7:30? Are you crazy?! I never see that hour unless I'm coming home from a party. You expect me to be awake after that? Oh my God. What have you done?! I can't do this job! You're gonna have to tell them no. Yes, you. I mean, it's your fault. You're the one who suckered me into this job. You're the one who said, "Sure, she'd love to do it." I never agreed to that. Man. And I actually thought you were my friend.

It's a Living

On the way to her friend's house, Cori has a bizarre encounter with a very strange man. She has just arrived at her friend's house.

Cori: You won't believe what just happened to me! I'm getting off the El and this guy comes up to me and says, "Hi there. You got a minute?" I say, "Sorry, I don't have any money," and I start to walk away. He scurries up beside me and goes, "Wait! I don't need any money. Actually I'm on my way to Crobar. It's fetish night." I pick up my pace. Then he runs in front of me, blocking my path and says, "Look, I don't mean to bug you and I'm not going to hurt you. It's just that I couldn't help but notice your beautiful feet in those sandals. I'll give you ten dollars if you let me smell them for just thirty seconds." You should have seen his face! The guy was dead serious! *(Beat.)* Of course I didn't! Are you kidding? *(Beat.)* I made him give me twenty.

Commission Mission

COMEDIC

Cheryl was shopping in the mall when she was approached by a commission-hungry salesgirl who was getting on her nerves. Cheryl decided to annoy the salesgirl in return. But now she needs her friend, Ann, to fix the situation.

Cheryl: I'm in the mall and I go into Merry-Go-Round, just to check out what new clothes they got in, right? Well, as soon as I walk in the store, this girl with huge hair and way too much make-up on rushes up to me and says, "Can I help you?" I say, "No thanks. I'm just looking." So she says, "Well, if you need anything, just holler." Obviously, somebody works on commission. I'm looking around and she keeps watching me and smiling like she's my new best friend. I was so annoyed. I wanted to choke her with her hair. But I refrained. I pick out five of the most expensive items in the store and bring them to the counter. The total comes to $815, and the cashier asks, "Did anyone help you today?" I say, "Yeah," and point to some guy who's goofing off in the corner. You should have seen Miss Smiley Face! It was great! But Ann, you've got to return everything for me. I mean, what am I going to do with five prom dresses?!

Ring of Lies

COMEDIC

Carol's friend Kate is a mess because her boyfriend just broke up with her. Carol tries to comfort Kate and cheer her up.

Carol: What a jerk! I can't believe he just dumped you like that after three years! Oh Kate, I'm so sorry. I know how much you love him. But you can do so much better. He doesn't deserve to be with you. Hey, come on now. Things could always be worse. He could have cheated on you. *(Beat.)* He didn't?! What a scumbag! Well, he could have asked for the ring back. *(Beat.)* That cheap son of a bitch. Oh, don't cry, don't cry — I'm thinking. Hey, at least you're not pregnant! *(Beat.)* Oh, no.

Dodging the Shadow

COMEDIC

Tessa is fed up with and jealous of her friend who always has to outshine her. Tessa finally confronts her, knowing her friend can't possibly top her this time.

Tessa: You do too! Every time I tell you some good news about something I did or something that happened to me, you always have to try to top me. Like the time David finally asked me out. You responded with how Mark wooed you to dinner with roses. Oh, and when I told you I lost five pounds, remember? You made me watch you weigh yourself, just to prove to me that you lost eight. Well you won't outshine me this time. Because I just got cast as Lady Macduff in Macbeth! What are you gonna say now? That you got Lady *Macbeth*? *(Beat.)* You got Lady Macbeth?! I hate you. I really, really hate you.

Critical Opinions

COMEDIC

Nicole is very insecure about her looks — especially her weight. She is getting ready for a party and asks her boyfriend how her outfit looks.

Nicole: Okay, how does this look? *(Beat.)* Are you sure? I mean, they said to dress casual, so I thought, this is pretty casual. You don't think it's too casual, do you? *(Beat.)* Good. Is it too dressy? *(Beat.)* Okay. Do I look fat? *(Beat.)* Oh my God, Jeff! *(Beat.)* No you didn't say "no," you said, "Uh, no." Uh is a pretty loaded word! It means, "Yes, you look like a bloated pig, only I better not tell you that!" Why didn't you just say, "Nicole, you ought to lie down on a silver platter with an apple shoved in your mouth?!" Ya know what? Forget it — I'm not going. I don't need people trying to pop me with toothpicks! *(Beat.)* Liar. *(Beat.)* Really? Are you sure? I mean, really, really, absolutely, positively, no-doubt-in-your-mind that I don't look fat? *(Beat.)* Okay. Jeff? Does my hair look all right?

Networking

Barbara's auditions have not been going very well. Before auditioning for another agent, Barbara consults her friend Kim, who tells her to be more assertive. After the audition, Barbara returns to tell Kim how it went.

Barbara: Yes, I did take your advice. I was much more assertive with this agent. I initiated the handshake, I maintained eye contact, I even spoke of my accomplishments more boldly. I did a monologue and read two commercials — and I was centered, focused, emotionally connected. Afterwards, she sat me down and told me that I was very talented, had a beautiful face, and she thought she could get me a lot of work. Then she added, "Get anorexic." Anorexic! Not drop 10 pounds, not tone-up! Get anorexic! Do you realize anorexia is a life-threatening disease?! So I said, "And why don't you call me when you've got cancer." And I gathered my things and walked out. *(Beat.)* You know, Kim, I really don't think assertiveness is my problem.

Award winner: Comedy Monologue Competition, International Modeling & Talent Association, Los Angeles 1999 & New York 1999 Conventions.

Busting Out

A friend is jealous of Andrea's big boobs. Here, Andrea lets her in on the downside of having a large chest.

Andrea: Okay. I admit there are some advantages to having boobs as big as mine. When I walk into a room, all male heads turn, and eyes lower about a foot. Plus they make a great storage area. Do you know that I can hold the TV Guide under one boob and the remote under the other? It's true. But there are lots of things you're not considering. You get to wear pretty, lacy bras. I have to buy mine at "Steel Cages Are Us." And at least you can do aerobics. The last time I jumped rope, my bra strap snapped in half and I had an odd-shaped black and blue mark on my cheek for days! Oh, and gravity is fun. The last guy I fooled around with couldn't wait to get my bra off. Then when he did, he was groping around in the dark trying to find them until I finally blurted out, "They're under my armpits, okay?!" Never saw him again. So stop feeling depressed, and thank God that when you take your bra off, you don't have to worry about stepping on your nipples!

Award winner: Comedy Monologue Competition, International Modeling & Talent Association, Los Angeles 2000 Convention.

The Gift

COMEDIC

Chrissy found a woman's Amoco credit card inside the door to her own gas tank. She has been using it to pay for her gas. Chrissy finally tells her best friend about it. Her friend is worried and cannot believe what Chrissy has been doing. Here, Chrissy tries to justify her actions.

Chrissy: What? It's not like I stole it. There I was parked at the Amoco gas pump with the last three dollars to my name. And I open the little door to the gas tank, and **boom** there it was. Tucked right in. Don't you see? The gas card was meant for me to have — maybe from some higher power — because I'm totally broke, and God wanted to help. It was a gift. You don't refuse gifts from God. That's rude. Worse you could be damned to hell. Besides, it's not like gas is something you own or wear. You just put it in your car and it goes. You shouldn't have to pay for that. Ya know, you're not going to make me feel guilty, Mary. The woman isn't going to have to pay for it. It's Amoco! They have money! And didn't they kill some animals in some oil spill once? This is like their payback. Anyway, it's over. The machine sucked it up. And I really don't think there's anything to worry about. *(Beat.)* Do you?

Breeding Ground

COMEDIC

Vicky has come to a community counseling center to see a therapist. It is not an upscale facility. She checks in with the receptionist, who tells her to have a seat. Vicky has a problem with that.

Vicky: Excuse me. I know you told me to have a seat, but did you notice that all of the chairs in this room are fabric? Not vinyl — fabric. Don't you realize that fabric chairs are not sanitary? There could be lice or crabs or God knows what else crawling around in those cushions! You could at least offer me some Saran wrap. And what's more, they stink! Can't you smell that foul odor wafting this way? It's disgusting! Don't your patients bathe? Hang a sign, "Have you showered today? If not — go home!" Look, I am here to see a therapist. To talk about my issues. And believe me, I have issues. But meanwhile, *meanwhile*, you are subjecting me to worse emotional trauma over this God-forsaken pit of a waiting room! Now, what are you going to do about it? *(Beat.)* Okay, I'm sitting, I'm sitting! *(She slowly sits down, looking grossed out, then pinches her nose.)* This is criminal.

Award winner: Comedy Monologue Competition, International Modeling & Talent Association, New York 1999 Convention.

Have You Gone Mad?

COMEDIC

Tanya's roommate (or friend) asks her to go to the grocery to get some Tide. Tanya returns empty-handed after having a strange and irritating experience. Her roommate/friend is upset that Tanya didn't get her the Tide. Tanya sets her straight.

Tanya: Ohhhh, no. Don't even go there. You have no idea what I have just been through. I'm in the grocery store looking for *your* laundry detergent and — big sign — Tide's on sale. Cool. But I'm looking and the shelf is like empty. Then I spot one last bottle. Well, I'm about to take it and this woman comes barreling down the aisle and snatches it up right under my nose. Man, was I pissed. So I go up behind her, grab it out of her greedy, little hands, and say, "Excuse me, but that's my Tide." Well she starts chasing me up and down the aisles as if I kidnapped her son! Finally, I stop and say, "Lady, what is your problem?" Well, she starts crying and carrying on — like she's going for an Oscar. So, just to shut her up, I say, "Here. Take the damn thing." So don't even give me that, "You forgot my Tide." From now on — get your own groceries!

Award winner: Comedy Monologue Competition, International Modeling & Talent Association, New York 1998 Convention.

Going For Broke

COMEDIC

Jeanine and her roommate have just returned from shopping. Her roommate thinks Jeanine spent far too much money that she doesn't have. She refers to Jeanine as the "privileged poor." Jeanine does not take this comment lightly.

Jeanine: The privileged poor?! Who are you talking about? I grew up in Cherry Hill — JAPVILLE, USA — home of the Mercedes. My father's vice president of Mobil Oil. I am not poor! I refuse. Besides, I don't know what you're worrying about. I didn't buy anything that we didn't put on our list in the first place. Look. We got the lamp, we got the matching towels for the bathroom — on sale — the shower curtain, and the futon. Aside from the diamond ring, I didn't buy a thing that wasn't on the list. And that's only 16 payments of $69.00 dollars a month. With no interest. Big deal. That's nothing. That's a third of my cell phone bill. And don't start on that. I need that for emergencies. What does that saying mean anyway—privileged poor? Isn't that an oxymoron? Or is that just what you're being? *(Beat.)* Hey, where are you going? *(Beat.)* You can't go shopping, we're broke. *(Beat.)* I said broke, not poor. There's a difference.

The Homecoming Queen

COMEDIC

Liz has not been having much luck with men, no matter how hard she tries. Here, she runs into an old friend from school.

Liz: Hillary? Hillary Bloomberg? I thought that was you! It's Liz — Simmons, remember? Yes! Wow, look at you! You look great! I mean, you really look great. How come you look so great? I eat like a bird, work-out four times a week, get facials regularly, and look at you. What's your secret? *(Beat.)* Engaged? Really? Congratulations. I bet he's a wonderful guy too, huh? How about that? You meet a man and feel happy, so now you look great. I'm trying to look great, so I can meet a man and feel happy. Isn't life funny? Yeah. Well, I gotta run, but tell Prince Charming, if he happens to know any frogs, send 'em my way. Tadpoles even. I'm really not that picky.

Bite-wings For Breakfast

COMEDIC

Sharon got into a fight with her boyfriend last night. Today at work, as a dental assistant, she discovered a new way to work out her anger. It is after work, and she is talking to her boyfriend.

Sharon: I've forgiven you. I mean it. I am completely over everything. I was working today and Susan, the other dental assistant, called in sick. It was like destiny smiling at me. What I mean is, I got to work with every single patient today! Do you know there is nothing more satisfying than yanking out people's teeth? I kept picturing each patient was you, and I was pulling, twisting, ripping out teeth left and right! The more they bled, the happier I felt! Then I started using the suction — sucking up people's tongues — making them twitch and jump! It was great! *I was in control.* I know they couldn't really feel anything. But the *thought* that I could be hurting them — inflicting severe, unbearable pain — was almost...orgasmic! So honey, I'm not mad at you anymore. Oh, and guess what? Dr. Greene said we could squeeze you in tomorrow. Isn't that great?!

Award winner: Comedy Monologue Competition, International Modeling & Talent Association, Los Angeles 1999 Convention.

The Hypochondriac

COMEDIC

Marlene's best friend is a hypochondriac and she's driving Marlene crazy with her latest fear.

Marlene: So you have a bump. It's an itsy, bitsy, teeny, little bump. Enough with the bump! You know, you're going to turn into an old lady if you keep this up. First with the shooting arthritis, then the case of the ingrown hair, now it's the infamous bump! You are driving both of us crazy! Let it go. Your hand is normal. Trust me. Look, my hand looks exactly…Oh my God, I have a bump too! You bumped me! Get the medical book. Hurry up, it could be spreading!

Award winner: Comedy Monologue Competition, International Modeling & Talent Association, Los Angeles 1999 & New York 1999 Conventions.

Midnight Parking

COMEDIC

Paula has been driving around her block looking for a parking spot for over an hour. Finally, she sees someone pulling out and turns on her blinker. Before she can park, a woman quickly backs her car into Paula's spot. Paula is livid.

Paula: Excuse me Ma'am, but I was here first. Waiting for that parking spot. See my car, right there, in the middle of the street? Notice how the left blinker is flashing? That means I was going to turn. Into this spot! And I would be parked right now if you hadn't come screeching backwards like a mad woman. *(Beat.)* Don't speak, just listen. I have been driving up and down these streets for over an hour. I am irritated. I am exhausted. I would like to go home and sleep. Look up there. See that apartment on the second floor? The one with all the lights out? Do you know why it's all dark? Because I am not in it! Stop! Don't even think of walking away. If you take so much as one more step I'm going to get back in my car, put it in reverse, and slam it into yours! Do you understand? *(Beat.)* Thank you. You're an angel.

Award winner: Comedy Monologue Competition, International Modeling & Talent Association, Los Angeles 2000 Convention.

Chocolate Sanity

COMEDIC

Joan is in a restaurant. She has PMS. She is having a major chocolate craving and just ordered dessert. The waiter brings her carrot cake by mistake. She is not happy, to say the least.

Joan: What is this? Carrot cake? I ordered the chocolate passion kiss. *(Beat.)* You most certainly did not because I never *distinctly* said anything involving carrots for you to *distinctly* hear. This is dessert! Who wants vegetables in it?! I want what I ordered and I told you what I ordered and that's what I want and I want it now. I want my chocolate kassion piss! — Stop laughing. You are a complete idiot of a waiter. Listen carefully. There are three letters that can bring you unbearable suffering. We're talking way beyond IRS, baby, and much more dangerous than STD. Those three little letters are PMS! *(Beat.)* On the house? *(Touched.)* I…I don't know what to say. *(Fighting tears.)* You have got to be the sweetest man I've ever met in my entire life. I'm sorry, I'm just…are you single?

Award winner: Comedy Monologue Competition, International Modeling & Talent Association, Los Angeles 2000 Convention.

FEMALE
MONOLOGUES

DRAMATIC

Quiet Heroes

Melissa is constantly getting picked on by a boy named Chuck. Everyone is afraid of him. Today, before school started, Chuck was teasing her again and Richie stood up to him. Chuck punched Richie in the eye, but Richie still stood his ground. It is now after school and Melissa approaches Richie.

Melissa: Richie, are you okay? Oh no, your eye's all swollen up. I hope it doesn't hurt too bad. I wanted to thank you for sticking up for me today. Chuck is always making fun of me. He hates me because he asked me out before and I said no. I didn't mean to hurt his feelings, I just didn't want to be his girlfriend. But now he wants to get back at me. He always calls me names in front of everyone so they won't like me. You're the first person who ever stood up to him. You were really brave. Nobody's ever done anything like that for me. I'm real sorry about your eye. But in a way, it makes you look cool — kinda tough, ya know? Um, I'm going to watch the game tomorrow and I was wondering…well, if you're not busy, do you want to go with me? *(Beat.)* Really? Great! So, I'll see you there tomorrow then. Richie? Thanks.

The Thorn Garden

Maria can't stand living at home anymore. Her father won't let her see her boyfriend, and she believes that her parents don't love her. She has decided to run away from home. Before leaving, she says good-bye to her younger sister, Rose.

Maria: No, no, it's not your fault. Rose, you're the best sister anyone could ever wish for. You are. It's Mom and Dad. Everything I do is wrong in their eyes. Dad hates every boyfriend I've ever had. He won't let me near Alberto. He said if he ever caught me with him again, he'd kill him. Alberto never did anything wrong. He loves me. And Mom just agrees with everything Dad says. She won't even listen to me. That's why I have to leave. I can't live like this. They don't love me. They never have. I have to go now. Please, don't cry. Be brave. I'll see you again, real soon. I promise. Rose? I love you more than anyone in the whole world. Don't ever forget that.

Inside These Walls

DRAMATIC

Pam's father is physically abusive to her and her mother. After being beaten by her father tonight, Pam runs to her friend's house in the hope of sleeping there. She is ashamed to tell her friend what just happened.

Pam: Hi. I'm sorry to bother you so late but, um, I was wondering if I could sleep over. *(Beat. She tries to cover the bruise on her cheek.)* Nothing happened. I just…tripped. Talk about stupid. But I'm fine. Really. I just don't feel like staying at my house tonight. *(Beat.)* Because it's, boring, you know? I thought it would be fun to stay at your place on a school night. What do you say? *(Beat.)* No, don't ask your mom! She'll call my parents! My dad said I could come! He doesn't care. He doesn't care at all! He's…drunk and he.. he slapped me and shoved me against the wall real hard. He hit my mom too. Don't make me go back there! I'm too scared. I'll be real quiet — I promise. I won't make a sound.

Etched in Stone

DRAMATIC

Shawn's parents recently got divorced because her father cheated on her mother. Shawn lives with her mom, but spends weekends at her dad's apartment. Shawn hates sitting around there on the weekends and asks her dad if she can go out with her friends. He calls her selfish and says that she doesn't care about her family.

Shawn: Selfish? I'm selfish? How can you say that? Just because I want to go out with my friends instead of sitting around your apartment feeling sorry for you? You always do that. Anytime I want to go out, you tell me how mean and selfish I am. How I don't care about the family. But you're the one who cheated on Mom. You're the one who ripped our family apart. But you can't bear to face that. So instead, you put all of your guilt and shame on me. God, is it any wonder that I hate coming here on weekends? And it's *not* because I don't care about the family. It's because you make me feel so mean and bad, that I wanna get away. Can't you once stop thinking about yourself and realize that the things you say about me, Dad, make me feel like I'm the most horrible person who ever lived. Why do you do that? Why do you hate me so much?

A Million Stars

Emily and Steven are girlfriend and boyfriend. Emily is a virgin. They have been fooling around in Steven's car. When Steven tries to go further, Emily pulls away and gets out of the car. Steven loves Emily and can't understand why she doesn't want to do it. Here, she discloses her feelings.

Emily: Because it just doesn't feel right. It's like all rushed and weird. This isn't the way I pictured it at all. I thought it would be somewhere nice. Not the back seat of your car. I want it to be romantic. I've held out for so long because it's a big deal to me. I'm practically the only girl in school who's still a virgin. All my friends keep teasing me about it. But I don't care what they say. Most of them just did it to get it over with. They didn't even like it — or the guy they did it with. I want it to be special. Something I'll remember for the rest of my life. I really like you, Steven. I want it to be with you. I do. But I think we should wait. This doesn't feel like the right time or place. And I don't want to regret doing it. Okay?

Freeing Impact

Robin recently started dating a guy that she really likes. Tonight, when he tries to kiss her, she pulls away. He is confused and hurt and thinks that she doesn't really like him. Desperate to convince him that she cares about him, Robin bravely reveals a tragic incident that is the cause of her inability to be intimate.

Robin: It was Prom night, after the Prom, and Brian and I were gonna drive to the beach for the weekend. God, were we psyched. We got in his car and cranked the music up real loud. It was a beautiful night, the wind blowing against my face, and we were so happy, so free. He stopped at a light and turned and looked at me — the same way you did just now. Then he leaned over and started to kiss me. And before I knew — it happened so fast — a car — it smashed into Brian's side. His head hit the edge of the door — I heard this crack — and then everything blacked out. The next thing I remember, I woke up in the hospital with a mild concussion and a broken arm. Brian was dead. It's been almost a year and I still can't let anyone kiss me. I'm sorry. But I can't.

Crossroads

DRAMATIC

Denise's father left a few years ago due to her mother's overbearing, self-absorbed, and alcoholic behavior. Denise has not seen or heard from him since. Her mother treats her poorly and always demands to meet Denise's boyfriends, whom she belittles and scares away. When her mother wants to meet her current boyfriend, Denise finally stands up to her.

Denise: Why should I introduce him to you, Mom? So you can rip him to shreds the second he walks in the door? You've never once approved of anyone I've dated. What is it, Mom? They're too good for me? I'm too good for them? Or is it that you hate all men since Daddy left you? That's it, isn't it? You can't stand to see me happy with someone because you're alone. Well, you can't blame Dad for that one. You pushed him away every chance you got. With your parties and your drinking and yelling all the time. I wanted to run away too. And now he's gone — not just from you — but from me, Mom. And I'll never forgive you for that. I want my dad back, and it's too late. So don't even think for one minute that I'm going to let you drive my boyfriend away too. You choose to be alone. I don't.

Award winner: Drama Monologue Competition, International Modeling & Talent Association, Los Angeles 1999, New York 1999, & Los Angeles 2000 Conventions.

Freud Was A Fake

DRAMATIC

Dana has been skipping acting class ever since her teacher suggested that she may have been sexually abused. Today, Dana returns. Concerned, the instructor asks if she's okay and if she's been avoiding her.

Dana: Yes, I've been avoiding you. And with good reason. I mean, ever since we had that talk, my life has become totally screwed up. I can't stop crying all the time, I'm scared of everything, and my parents threatened to kick me out of the house 'cause I'm too emotional! I trusted you. And you put these ideas and fears in my head and I can't get them out! And then you said you'd be there for me. But when I came to you, you were too busy to even listen to me. Don't you understand? Every time I see you, it makes me think about all of these terrifying things inside me that I don't want to think about. In some strange way, I still really care about you. But right now, I can't even be in the same room with you. I'm sorry, but I just can't.

Wildwood

Stephanie has been saving money and making plans to spend the summer at the beach with some friends. She didn't want to bring it up with her father until they had found an apartment and she could show him that she saved up her own money. She finally asks her dad if she can go.

Stephanie: Oh, come on, Dad! It's only for the summer. I saved up the rent money and I'll get a job as soon as I get there. There are tons of jobs on the boardwalk. *(Beat.)* That's not fair! David got to go last summer. *(Beat.)* I know he's a boy — so what? I can take care of myself. I'm responsible. You're not even listening to me. Why are we having this talk if you already made up your mind and won't even hear me out? We already found a place — it's so nice. And I promise I'll be very careful and safe. Besides, what am I gonna do around here all summer? Please? *(Beat.)* Oh, that's great. Just walk away! Well, I'm going and you can't stop me. I'm not a baby anymore, Dad. *(Beat.)* Fine, if that's the way you want it, you got it. I *won't* come back. You'll be free of me at last. Just like you've always wanted.

Loving Tallie

DRAMATIC

Allison and Tallie are sisters. Tallie has been dating a guy named Gary. Last night at a party, Gary was hitting on Allison when Tallie wasn't in sight. It is the following evening and Tallie is getting ready to go out with Gary. Allison doesn't want to hurt Tallie's feelings, but decides she must tell her what happened.

Allison: That was some party last night, huh? I'm surprised you have the energy to head out again tonight. Are you going out with Gary? *(Beat.)* Tallie, I really don't think you should. *(Beat.)* Because…he was hitting on me last night. I know he was a little drunk, but he was all over me. I told him — I said, "What the hell's the matter with you? You're dating my sister!" And he goes, "You're just so beautiful, can you blame me?" *(Beat.)* Tallie, it's true! I am not jealous! My God! I know you think I always want every guy to like me, but that's not the case. Do you really think I'd want my own sister's boyfriend to be such a slime that he'd hit on me? This is not about competition or egos, Tallie. I care about you and I don't want to see you get hurt. I know you're afraid that Gary is the only guy who will ever like you, but you're so wrong. Tallie, you're beautiful — you are. And you're smart and funny and sweet. You can find someone else. Someone who's as special as you are.

Skin Deep

Jacquelyn's younger sister is upset because people, especially guys, always refer to her as cute. She wants them to think she is sexy or gorgeous, like they do about Jacquelyn. Here, Jacquelyn admits that it's not as great as her sister thinks.

Jacquelyn: There's nothing wrong with cute. I know, you want a guy to say you're gorgeous or sexy or hot. Well, you know what? That's what guys tell me all the time and I'm sick of it. When a guy says I'm sexy or gorgeous, all it means to me is that he's checked me out and he likes what he sees. Like I'm a piece of meat that turns him on, and all he wants is to sleep with me — and that's it. But cute is about you — your personality. It means you're adorable, sweet, cuddly, nice. I would give anything to be in your shoes. If just once a guy would tell me I was cute, then I'd know it was about me — on the inside. That he actually looked past my physical appearance and really thought that I was…lovable.

Between Us

Kathy is pregnant. Her mom is very upset and thinks Kathy should have an abortion because she's not ready for the responsibility. Hurt and confused, Kathy turns to her sister, Krista, for advice.

Krista: I know the things Mom said make it sound like she thinks you're not responsible enough to have a baby. I hear you. I know she's been yelling and acting crazy. But trust me, it's not because she thinks you're incapable or too screwed up. It's because she's worried about you. If she didn't love you, she wouldn't be so angry and stubborn — she simply wouldn't care. Think about it. You're her daughter, you're not with the father, and it takes a lot of time and money and sacrifices to raise a baby. *(Beat.)* No, no! I'm not agreeing with her that you should have an abortion. Look, I've listened to everything you've said about making this decision. But the thing is, I can't tell you what to do. This is your life, Kathy. All I can tell you is what I hear you saying. And what I hear is that you couldn't live with yourself if you didn't have the baby. Don't choose based on what Mom or anyone else thinks you should do. Trust yourself. Listen to your heart.

A Safe Place

Jodi's younger sister, Karen, is dating a man who is obsessive, jealous, and abusive. Earlier tonight, he hit Karen. Luckily, Jodi was there to call the police, who put him in jail for the night and suggested that Karen sign a restraining order. Jodi left the room to call the boyfriend's parents while Karen finished up with the police. The cops have gone, and Karen has just admitted to Jodi that she didn't sign it.

Jodi: What?! Why didn't you sign it? That restraining order means he can never come near you again. By law. Karen, look at me. I know you care about him and you don't want to hurt him, but look what he's done to you. That's not love. It's obsession. He's hit you twice already. Do you really think he's going to stop now? Listen to me. You're my baby sister. I've protected you your whole life. You've seen how crazy I get if anyone hurts you in the slightest way. It's because I love you more than anything in this world. But what if I wasn't here tonight? What if something…really bad happened to you? I couldn't live without you Karen. Sign the restraining order. Please. If you can't do it for you, I beg you, sign it for me.

In Through the Out Door

DRAMATIC

Shelley and her boyfriend just had a bad argument. As usual, he heads for the door. Shelley makes a final attempt to save their relationship.

Shelley: Go ahead! Just walk out like you always do whenever we have a fight! You're too scared to stay and talk about it. *(Beat.)* Then why are you running away? It doesn't make anything better. You'll still have to sit with all of your feelings. They won't go away until you get them out. Talk to me. Yell at me — cry to me. Anything! Just please don't leave me again. Not like this. If we can't communicate with each other, it's never going to work. And if that's how it's always going to be, tell me now and I'll let you go. Because I can't take this anymore. It hurts too much.

Breaking the Silence

Sarah is scared to tell her family something about herself. She's afraid they won't love her anymore. They are old fashioned and seem to be living perfect lives. Here, her good friend Gina tries to convince her that she shouldn't be ashamed to tell them. (The secret that Sarah fears telling them has been deliberately left open for the actor.)

Gina: That is bullshit. I can't believe that you can't see that. Of course I don't know your family as well as you do, but I don't have to. You think just because they're Catholic and your sisters and brothers are happily married and your parents are old and conservative that they've never done anything wrong? Listen to yourself. "Ask anyone who knows them, they're the all-American, good, moral family." And I'm not saying they aren't kind, loving people. I'm saying they've all done things they're ashamed of, Sarah. They all have their own deep, dark secrets. Because they're human. Humans aren't perfect. If you could drop your need to defend them and believe that, you wouldn't be so frightened to let them know the real you. Don't live in fear of their disapproval — tell them. Trust me, Sarah, they won't stop loving you.

Award winner: Drama Monologue Competition, International Modeling & Talent Association, Los Angeles 1999 Convention.

Beyond Wonderland

DRAMATIC

Simone has been dating someone who keeps leading her on and then blowing her off. He's like Dr. Jekyll and Mr. Hyde. Unfortunately, she has really fallen for him. About a week ago, she drove a long way to see him in a show. She waited for him after the show until she was the last person there. He was gone. Today, out of nowhere, he shows up at her door.

Simone: What are you doing here? Wait — let me guess. You haven't heard from me in a week so you thought you'd better show up to make sure I'd still be thinking about you. Don't look at me like that. You know exactly what I'm talking about. I'm so sick of your games. I drive all the way out to see your show and you sneak out of the theatre without even saying hi. You weren't looking for me like you claimed because you would have seen me — I was there. Then you don't e-mail me for days. And just when I'm about to say the hell with you, you call and leave a message like nothing ever happened. I have feelings, ya know. I'm not a toy for you to play with when you get the urge to be entertained. Jesus, I hate you right now. And I hate me too. For being dumb enough to *still* not be able to get you out of my head. Don't. Don't say anything. It'll just make things worse. And I can't handle anymore. I can't.

Award winner: Drama Monologue Competition, International Modeling & Talent Association, Los Angeles 2000 Convention.

Good Enough

Rachel has been working as a bankcard salesperson for the past six months. The job has her working around the clock, completely stressed out, and getting sick every month. Finally, she decides that although she has nothing else lined up, she needs to quit. She has just announced that she quit her job to her roommate, Ann, who is instantly upset and worried that Rachel won't be able to pay the rent.

Rachel: What do you mean, "How could you do that?" I had to quit my job. You know how miserable and stressed out I've been the past six months. I've been sick half the time I've worked for that damn bank. Did you want me to end up buried alive under all that depression and paper work? I know you're worried that I won't be able to pay my share of the rent, but Jesus, Ann, what about my sanity? My health? I thought you'd be happy for me that I finally got out of that hell-hole. Of all people, I expected you to be the one to support me and say I did the right thing. But no, all you can do is think about yourself. Well, don't worry, Ann, I'll get the rent money. Even if I have to beg my father. You'll be just fine. As always.

Award winner: Drama Monologue Competition, International Modeling & Talent Association, Los Angeles 1999 Convention.

The Runaway

DRAMATIC

Crystal has had several bad relationships with men. She always winds up getting hurt. She has recently been dating a guy who she's really starting to like, but she is so afraid of getting hurt again, she tries to push him away.

Crystal: Take the roses back! I don't want 'em. You keep givin' me all these things and takin' me out to dinner and actin' all sweet. Don't think I don't know what you're tryin' to do. Quit lookin' at me like that! Man, I keep pushin' and pushin' you away, and you keep comin' back like some little puppy dog. What's the matter with you? Can't you take a hint? Why don't you go away? *(Beat.)* No. Don't say that. You don't love me! Guys always pull that crap and the next thing I know…Look, I've been around the block, okay? And every time I get burned. Every time. I don't need that again, thank you. So just do me a favor and leave now before somethin' messed up happens. I mean it. Go. I hate you! I hate you! Cause I'm fallin' for you, and I'm scared, okay? *(Beat.)* I'm scared to death that you're gonna hurt me.

Just Friends

Sheila's best friend fell in love with her. After many awkward months, he finally got over her, and their friendship became stronger than ever. They decided to move into an apartment together to save on rent money. Before signing the lease, Sheila asked him about any lingering romantic feelings toward her, and he assured her there were none. They have been settling into their new apartment for a week when he admits that he is still in love with her. Sheila is understandably upset.

Sheila: No, don't say that! Not now! We already talked this out two weeks ago. You said you were over me — that you didn't feel that way anymore. Why, why did you lie to me? I believed you or I never would have agreed to move in with you. Now what are we supposed to do? Your timing is unbelievable. We just signed the lease — it's too late to back out now. Look, I don't mean to hurt you, you're my best friend. But it's not fair to me. I don't want that pressure and awkwardness. How am I supposed to feel comfortable when Ryan comes over? *(Beat.)* No — don't be sorry — it doesn't help. You always do that. You want me to forgive you immediately so *you* can feel better. Well what about *me*? I'm allowed to feel my feelings. I'm entitled to be mad. It doesn't mean I'll stop caring about you. It'll pass. But right now, I need to be alone. Please, just let me be alone.

The Crossing Guard

DRAMATIC

Diana was physically and sexually abused as a child. As a result, relationships with men have always been difficult. She loves her boyfriend and has been more open and trusting with him than any past boyfriend, but sometimes she still gets scared and pushes him away. She has just done it again. Her boyfriend thinks she doesn't really love him and is about to call it quits. He doesn't know about her abuse. Diana is too frightened to come right out and tell him, so she uses a metaphor instead.

Diana: There was this little girl who was walking across the street — *(Beat.)* It has everything to do with us if you'd just listen. She was walking across the street and she got hit by some drunk man in this beat-up, old truck. He slammed into her so hard that her body rolled over the truck and landed on the pavement behind him. It took her years to recover and find the courage to even stand at the curb again. Well, there you are on one side of the street, and I'm on the other. And all you can see is that I'm not standing next to you. But I want so badly to trust that you won't hurt me, to be with you, that I've managed to walk halfway across that street. If you'd stop for one minute to consider how hard — how terrifying that is for me, there'd be no way you could ever doubt that I love you.

Behind the Mask

DRAMATIC

Natalie both idolizes and envies Jessica because Jessica is bold, brave, and popular with men. Upset, Natalie tells Jessica how much she looks up to her and wishes she could be like her. Jessica admits that she is not everything Natalie thinks she is.

Jessica: It's all fake, Natalie. It's always been fake. I'm just good at it. I can make anyone think I'm strong — invincible — so they all back down from me. And the men? They don't really like me. They just *think* they do because I know exactly how to look at them, to play the game, to seduce them. So, lucky me, they all want to screw me. And the ones who fall for me — it's only cause I'm a challenge. I put myself up on this pedestal and keep them down below. Everyone thinks I'm so confident, brave, so together. It's all a lie, to keep me safe. The truth is I'm so lonely and scared that I hate myself. Because I know, deep down, there is no way anyone could ever love me — behind the facade. And that makes me feel so crazy and sick inside that I want to kill myself. So here's your idol, Natalie. Still wanna be like me?

Award winner: Drama Monologue Competition, International Modeling & Talent Association, Los Angeles 1999 & New York 1999 Conventions.

Tigers

DRAMATIC

Lauren has just returned from a vacation. She has missed her boyfriend and is eager to see him. However, when they get together, something seems to be bothering him. She asks him what is wrong, and he admits that he slept with someone while she was away. Lauren is shocked, angry, and heartbroken.

Lauren: Why? No, tell me. I want to know. Why did you do it? What was it you found so irresistible about her, that it was worth throwing our relationship away? Was she prettier than me? Did she have a Playboy body? Or was she just an easy lay? *(Beat.)* Why should I stop? I'm trying to come up with a good excuse for you. Only, I'm not finding any. There are no good reasons. Except one. You never really loved me. It was all a game — just a bunch of lies to make me fall for you so you wouldn't be lonely. When I think of the train ride to Boston and the night on the overpass, or the day at the zoo...that was another person. It had to be. Because I loved that man and he loved me. And he would never ever break my heart, the way you did just now.

The Light at the End of the Tunnel

DRAMATIC

Jane was sexually abused by her grandfather when she was a child. The abuse was so traumatic that she blocked it from her memory. Years later, she began to have panic attacks and flashbacks. As she recalled the abuse, her world turned upside down, and she spent many years in therapy. She has recently decided to sue her grandfather. Here, she finally confronts him about what he did to her.

Jane: Shut up! That's right, Grandpa, I said shut up. For once you are going to listen to me. You can pretend to everyone else how kind and sweet and generous you are, but not to me. It won't work anymore, because I know what you did to me and I know damn well you know it too. But what you can never know is how badly you fucked up my entire life. I was just a little girl and I trusted you. I even loved you. And now I'm a grown woman who's afraid of the dark, afraid to go into the bathroom alone, afraid to have sex or get close to a man because of you. But that's all changing as of this moment. Because I am here to tell you that I'm taking my power back. Do you hear me? I'm not a helpless child anymore and you will never, ever touch me or anyone else again. You got that? I'll see you in court, Grandpa.

Award winner: Drama Monologue Competition, International Modeling & Talent Association, Los Angeles 1999 Convention.

Searching For Justice

Janis witnessed a man being brutally beaten. For the past two years, a private investigator has been periodically questioning her. Today she finally went to court to testify. She is outraged and devastated when the defendant is declared innocent. After the courtroom empties, she confronts the defendant's attorney.

Janis: Justice was served?! You've got to be kidding me! I was there. I saw everything. Your client beat that man to a bloody pulp. He left him lying in the street. Just a mass of blood where his face used to be. You saw the pictures. He had to have his entire face surgically redone. And why? Because your hero was itching for a fight and didn't like his long hair. Two years of private investigators calling me and having me identify photos. And for what? So I could sit in that witness stand and have you twist my words into lies. You must be awfully proud of yourself. What do you feel when you're lying in bed at night? Do guilt or shame ever come creeping in? I have been waiting in that stuffy office all day. Because I came here to tell the truth. And I did. Now would you tell me something? How can you live with yourself? How?

MALE
MONOLOGUES

COMEDIC

Crushed

Justin has a major crush on a girl at school. She's so pretty and popular that he doesn't really think he stands a chance. Although he is incredibly nervous, he finally musters up the courage to ask her to go to a party with him.

Justin: Well…uh…Jimmy — ya know, Jimmy? He's having a party on Saturday. And…it sounds like it's gonna be really cool. So I was wondering…um…I know you and Kevin broke up — and I'm real sorry about that — but, uh…I was thinking, maybe — I mean if you're not busy — if you are I totally understand. But, well…what I'm trying to say is…would you…do you think…would you like to go with me? I don't mean go out-out. I mean the party. Jimmy's. *(Beat.)* Really?! Great! Uh, er, cool. So I'll see you — I mean I'll call you to…ya know — Saturday. Okay, bye. *(Beat.)* Oh my God! Breathe idiot, breathe!

Award winner: Comedy Monologue Competition, International Modeling & Talent Association, Los Angeles 2000 Convention.

Massive High

COMEDIC

It is the day before Cody and his best friend start high school. Suddenly, his friend becomes quite worried. Here, Cody attempts to psych him up and rid him of his fears.

Cody: Nervous? Don't be nervous. What's there to be nervous about? We've been waiting to start high school for like ever. It's gonna be so awesome! Just think how many mega-babes are gonna be walking through those halls and in our classes! And we'll finally have bigger lockers and a decent gym and multiple floors! Just like a mall! And tons of people to meet, parties to get invited to, real football games, new teachers who don't hate us yet! New faces everywhere you look! It's huge! I mean, we probably won't even see each other *(Realizing as he speaks.)* the whole…day…long. *(Beat.)* You're still gonna eat lunch with me, right?

Winning Stephanie

COMEDIC

Ricky is dying to go out with Stephanie. Stephanie has just told him that Evan Coleman asked her out. Ricky desperately tries to win her over.

Ricky: Evan Coleman?! Stephanie, you do not want to go out with him. Trust me. Did you know that he bites his toenails and spits them out? I'm serious — I know. We shared a bunk at summer camp. *(Beat.)* Okay, it was 5th grade — but still, who's to say he ever stopped? Habits like that are not easy to break. Do you really want to kiss him knowing where his mouth is at night? Besides, everyone knows he just got dumped by Jenny Freemont. He's on the rebound, and you're his…bound, so to speak. He'll only use you and drop you the second Jenny wants him back. You deserve someone way better than that. *(Beat.)* Like…me, for example. I'm available. No rebound stuff going on here. And I've never, ever chewed my toenails. Not once. Steph, wait! I was just getting to my really good qualities!

Caught in a Funk

COMEDIC

Kyle's friend Tom recently got dumped by his girlfriend. Here, Kyle tries to cheer him up.

Kyle: Tom, you have got to get out of this funk. I know Christy dumped you and that really sucks. But you've gotta move on. She's just one girl — there are millions of 'em out there. C'mon, things could definitely be worse. Trust me, I know. Remember when I got hit in the eye with a golf ball and had to wear that patch? Everyone called me Popeye or The Retarded Pirate for months. Now that was devastating. Or how about when Wendy dumped me for my brother? Talk about suck-ola! That was betrayal times two! And just yesterday I found out that I failed English and I have to take the whole class over again. I flunked my own language! How pathetic is that? *(Beat.)* Well, that's great. I'm glad you feel better. Because I just thoroughly depressed myself.

In Deep

COMEDIC

Jake's parents insisted on signing him up for the swim team. Terrified, he desperately tries to convince the coach that it's all some huge mistake.

Jake: Coach, I know it's the first day of swim practice and my name's on the list, but that's a big mistake. I never even tried out. Do I look familiar? *(Beat.)* See! So I just wanted to let you know. See ya. *(Beat.)* What?! No way! Coach, I can't. I know my parents called and signed me up, but they were having a psychotic episode. Thank God they're okay now — back to normal. They even asked me to come and tell you it was a freak accident. You see, they forgot — I'm allergic to water. I can't even shower! Don't you smell my B.O.? I reek! Plus, I saw *Jaws* and I've been emotionally scarred ever since. I mean, if he could get into that shallow bay area, he could definitely find his way into this pool! Besides, I forgot my suit. *(Beat.)* Really? Why didn't you tell me it was that easy?

The Wash Out

Dennis hasn't had much luck getting a date for the upcoming dance. When his friend asks about his love life, Dennis confesses it hasn't been going well.

Dennis: My love life? It's awesome. I mean, it's excellent. It's, it's so…it sucks. I asked three girls to the dance next weekend. Maria said no cause she's got a boyfriend in Italy that I didn't know about. Then I asked Tammy who said she'd die of an infectious disease before she'd go with me. I felt terrible. I didn't know she was sick. Finally, I asked June, but she said she had to wash her hair. I said, "Well, that's okay. I'll wash mine too. Then we'll go." But apparently her hair takes all night to wash. Who would've guessed cause she has really short hair, ya know? Talk about bad timing. Why couldn't she have been washing it Wednesday or Thursday instead? Well, I still have a few days left. Maybe I'll ask Stacey. I don't think she washes her hair.

Puberty Blues

After school, Brent's buddy wants to know if Brent went through with his plan to ask Heather out. Embarrassed, Brent confesses that he was almost ready to make his move when he totally humiliated himself.

Brent: I'm in English class today — the class Heather's in with me. And I'm all set to ask her out after class is over. Well, she keeps on staring at me. You know, real flirty like. I am pumped cause I can tell she really likes me. Just then, Mrs. Jordan asks who knows the difference between a metaphor and a simile. My hand shoots up. I'm thinking, "Cool. Here's my chance to show Heather that, not only am I a good-looking guy, but there's some awesome brain power going on inside." I start to say, "A metaphor is based on a resemblance of —" and it happens— *(Says with voice cracking.)* "a literal to an implied subject." Everybody starts laughing. It's like, suddenly, everyone, including Heather, is acutely aware of the fact that I'm sprouting hairs on my genitalia! I had to get out of there. So I ask to go to the bathroom and my voice cracks again! Heather was probably thinking, "He's going to measure it to see if it's grown!" I never went back. So to answer your question, no, I didn't have the balls to ask her out.

The Expert

Randy is buying condoms for the first time. To his embarrassment, the condoms are behind the counter, and an older woman is working at the register.

Randy: Yes, I need to get some *(Lowering voice.)* condoms. *(Beat. Clearing throat, louder.)* Condoms. *(Beat.)* Uh, what kinds have you got? I can't really see — I'm extremely nearsighted. *(Beat.)* Uh huh. Glow in the dark?! This isn't Halloween! I don't want to scare her, for God's sake! I think I'll go with the Trojans. *(Beat.)* No, I don't need the econo-pack. Not that I don't *need* it. I just prefer to buy them in small quantities. Ya know, keep 'em fresh. *(Beat.)* Size? Well, you better give me the extra large. *(Beat.)* Of course I'm sure. This isn't like the first time I've bought condoms or anything. I buy them all the time. Constantly. Sometimes twice a day. Not that I sleep around. I would never do that. It's just me and my girl. Uh, Ma'am? Do these come with directions?

Award winner: Comedy Monologue Competition, International Modeling & Talent Association, Los Angeles 2000 Convention.

Little Magnets

COMEDIC

Joel heard from a dorky guy at school that he met girls when he took his little cousin to the beach. Joel figures if it can work for "Buttface," it can definitely work for him. The only problem is that he doesn't have a little sister or cousin. Here, Joel goes to his friend Barry's house in the hopes of borrowing Barry's little sister.

Joel: Hey Barry. I know you're busy studying for your geometry test, so I figured I'd stop by and offer to baby-sit Ashley for you. Free of charge. *(Beat.)* What do ya mean why? You're my friend. I know how bad you've gotta ace that test. What, I can't do you a favor? *(Beat.)* Okay, okay. You know Adam Bennett? Yeah, Buttface — that's him. He told me he took his little cousin to the beach yesterday, and she was like a chick magnet! All these girls kept coming over to talk to her, and he wound up getting three of their phone numbers! I mean, we're talking Buttface here! But hey, you know how chicks go crazy over cute, little kids. So, I was thinking — *(Beat.)* Aww, c'mon! Can't I just borrow her for a few hours? *(Beat.)* How about one hour — that's it — and I'll bring her back? *(Beat.)* I'll give you twenty bucks? *(Beat.)* Cool! Oh, one more thing. Do ya think you could study somewhere nearby in case she needs her diaper changed?

Award winner: Comedy Monologue Competition, International Modeling & Talent Association, Los Angeles 2000 Convention.

Heaven in 7-11

COMEDIC

On the way to his friend's house, Dustin stopped at 7-11 for a snack. He had an exciting encounter with a total babe who turned out to be more than he expected. Afterwards, he rushes to his friend's place to tell him what happened.

Dustin: Dude, you won't believe this. I'm in 7-11, checking out the munchies, when I look over and there's this totally hot girl. I'm like, "Whoa!" I mean, she had this long hair and her body was perfect. But she was probably, I don't know, 25. But she looks at me and smiles. Dude, I was so stoked! Well, not to look too obvious, I go and get a Slurpee. Then I slide in line behind her, but I'm playin' it cool. Just sucking on my Slurpee, real casual, ya know? She pays for her stuff and turns to me and says, "You've got some on your lip." And she takes her finger and wipes the Slurpee off my mouth, then puts it in *her* mouth! Then she smiles and walks out. Dude!! I drop my Slurpee — it's everywhere, the cashier's bitchin'. I run out after her like "Wait!" I look, and she's got a car full of kids. And she leans over to the little girl and wipes some food off her face and then puts it in her mouth. And it hits me. She wasn't picking me up — she was cleaning me off! Ya know, Mommying me! Talk about twisted! Dude, it's a good thing I blew her off like I did or she probably woulda wanted to breast-feed me.

Foot in Mouth

Jordan's girlfriend Jessica recently broke up with him because he blew her off to spend the night at Carrie Benson's house. Jordan and Carrie are good friends. Jessica has been avoiding him ever since. Here, he tries to convince Jessica that nothing happened. But the harder he tries, the more his words come out wrong.

Jordan: Hey, Jessica. Oh, c'mon. Can't I talk to you for just a minute? Look, I know I was a jerk— *(Beat.)* Okay, a major jerk. And I don't blame you for dumping me. Well, just a little. Joke — that was a joke! I'm sorry I blew you off last Saturday. But the only reason I did was because Carrie Benson was upset about Doug breaking up with her. She was lonely, she needed a friend, and she promised me a good time. Jess, wait! That's not what I mean. I didn't sleep with her. She didn't want to. Hold up, hold up! That came out way wrong. What I'm trying to say is that she wanted me to spend the night, and I wanted to be with her. Not be with her, be with her! Don't you understand? Every time I think of you, that little four letter word keeps flooding my head. You know, the "L" word? Does that happen when you think of me? It does?! *(Beat.)* Liar? That wasn't exactly the word I had in mind.

Blowing a Kiss

COMEDIC

Rusty had an embarrassing experience with Janis over the weekend. Here, he confides in his friend Greg and asks for his advice.

Rusty: Greg? Have you talked to Janis today by any chance? *(Beat.)* Because, you know how much I like her, right? Well, we went to a party on Saturday night. And everything was going cool between us. She was definitely flirting with me, ya know? And we both got totally drunk. We were laughing so hard — it was great. So we wind up stumbling outside — just the two of us, alone. And I guess the beer kicked in cause I finally went for it. I started to kiss her. And the next thing I know, she pulls back and barfs all over the sidewalk! It's not funny! I kissed her and she puked! Talk about rejection. I mean, I've been blown off by girls before, but never so…thoroughly. Now I'm too embarrassed to even talk to her. So, seriously, what do you think? Did she have too much beer or was she playing really hard to get?

Double Vision

COMEDIC

Matt has been trying to get Laura to go out with him for a long time. She has finally agreed, on one condition: that they double date. Here, Matt tries to persuade his friend to go with them.

Matt: Take a chance, would ya?! Look, we've been friends for a long time, right? I wouldn't steer you wrong. This girl is gorgeous. I'm telling you — I met her. Legs to die for, a beautiful smile. She's smart, funny, and — get this — she loves sports! Where else are you going to find all that in one package? We're talking a rare commodity here. I'd ask her out myself, if I wasn't already crazy about Laura. It's one date. If you don't like her, which I doubt, you never have to see her again. *(Beat.)* Why? Because it will be fun. Because I know you'll like her…Because Laura won't go out with me alone. Oh c'mon! I need you, man! I mean I *neeeed* you. I'll let you drive my dad's new car? *(Beat.)* Great! See you at 8:00!

Award winner: Comedy Monologue Competition, International Modeling & Talent Association, Los Angeles 1999 Convention.

Where Envy Lies

COMEDIC

Keith is annoyed with a guy who thinks he's ultra cool. Here, Keith vents his disgust to a friend and tries to get him to agree that Mr. Cool is an irritating loser.

Keith: What a joke! Do you believe that guy? Mr. *I'm a stud.* And that, "Catch ya later, boys." Boys?! He's two years younger than we are. Who does he think he is? Slick, happenin' Granddad of the year? And those stupid-ass sunglasses. Have you ever seen him — even once — without them plastered to his face? There could be a thunderstorm at midnight and he'd still have them on. Whew, man, I can still smell him. He must have that Polo bottle stuffed inside his pants. I'm amazed he doesn't pass out from chemical poisoning. But did you see those two babes with him? They were hot! What the hell do they see in him? I mean, if you were a girl, would you actually date him? *(Beat.)* Okay, I know he's all muscles, but c'mon. *(Beat.)* Well, yeah, he's not ugly or anything. But his personality? *(Beat.)* On a good day, okay, he can be kinda funny. What? *(Beat.)* Yeah, I guess he is pretty cool, isn't he? Dammit! I hate that about him.

First Impressions

Here, Darren coaches his friend on how to pick up girls.

Darren: No, no, no, no. Man, you've got it all wrong. What's up with that slouched-over thing? Girls do not go for that. It makes you look like the hunchback. *(Imitating the Hunchback of Notre Dame.)* "Water, water!" Trust me man, it's not attractive. Look, ya gotta stand your ground — get centered. Now stick your chest out. I said *out*, dude. That's out? Okay, we'll work on that. Then, get your head up. Let 'em know you're confident, you're aware of your surroundings, you're lookin'. That's it. Now, the hands are very important. Right here. Not on your hips, Superman! Hey look, here comes two fine babes right now. Watch and weep. *(As they walk by.)* How ya doin', ladies? *(He looks embarrassed.)* Stop laughing! So I haven't perfected it yet, okay? Hey, show me that slouchy thing you do again. *(He imitates.)* Yeah, that's good.

Subtle Warnings

Tina is going out on a date with Jeremy for the first time. When Jeremy arrives to pick her up, he is greeted by Tina's overprotective brother, Carl. Carl, in his own charming and subtle way, warns Jeremy not to mess with his sister.

Carl: So you must be Jeremy. I'm Tina's brother Carl. It's nice to finally meet ya. Tina will be down in a minute. You know how girls are. So, it's the big first date, huh? Where are ya taking her? *(Beat.)* A party? All right. Sounds fun. Just between you and me, Jer, are there gonna be any drugs at this party? *(Beat.)* Just beer? That's cool. Ya know, Tina is such a lightweight. One beer and she'll be puking all over you. Not a pretty sight. So, you better keep her away from the alcohol. For the sake of your clothes, ya know? Tina told me you play soccer. Tough game. I'd play myself, but I've been studying Karate for years. I'm a 3rd degree black belt now. *(Beat.)* I love it, but sometimes I have to watch myself. Like say someone lays a hand on…Tina, for example. I could kill them instantly if I'm not careful. But otherwise, Karate's awesome. Well, it was cool meeting you. And hey, have fun on your date.

Getting In

COMEDIC

Patrick is a high school senior who has recently applied to college. He is nervously awaiting an answer from the one university that he has his heart set on. Meanwhile, his friends keep asking him if he got in, which is making Patrick feel even more pressure. When yet another friend casually asks Patrick if he got in, Patrick goes off on him.

Patrick: Did I get in? Did I get in—did I get in—did I get in!!! Do you have a death wish? How dare you ask me if I got in! Just who the hell do you think you are? My mother? Einstein? God? The future of my life depends on whether I get into this college, and you think I'm going to share that with you? Huh?! I haven't heard yet!! Okay?! You happy now? Are you satisfied? I haven't heard! I haven't…heard. Oh my God. Do you think that's a bad sign?

The Eternal Roommate

COMEDIC

Ray and Cliff are roommates. Cliff is studying for a big test he has tomorrow, when Ray comes home with a carful of friends and beer. Cliff asks Ray to talk privately. He is clearly upset and lets Ray know it. Here, Ray tries to justify the situation.

Ray: Cliff, hold up! I'm not trying to be a bad roommate here. I know you've gotta study. It's just, I was driving to the concert and outta nowhere — *(Makes tire blowing noise.)* — I get a flat. Right on Route 73! I was like the frog in Frogger. Somehow I manage to get to this Mom and Pop gas-station-repair-place, but they've got no tire for me. Go figure. I've gotta get to the concert, so I leave my car on some road and hitch a ride with this chick who's driving like ninety-five while getting stoned. Unbelievably, we make it there in one piece and I'm supposed to be meeting Candy and Courtney. I promised them a ride home. Suddenly I realize, I left my ticket in my car! I'm totally screwed! I start talking to the scalpers and this one girl swears I'm Jim Morrison and gives me a free ticket! Like, thanks, but put the pipe down! I practically miss the whole concert though, cause I'm searching for Candy and Courtney. Finally, I find them and tell them about my car. We're all three stranded now. Bing! I get a plan: Party at my place! Score — I got us all home! And I promise I'll kick 'em out in like 5 minutes so you can study. In the meantime, want a beer?

The Beacon

COMEDIC

Stuart and his college roommate made a pact when they first moved in together to warn each other when either of them had a girl over. The signal was to put a light in the dorm window. Last night, Stuart walked in on his roommate having sex. Appalled, he quickly left and spent the night on the couch in the dorm lounge. It is the next morning and the girl has left. Upset, Stuart confronts his roommate.

Stuart: Where was the signal? The signal. The third-day-we-moved-in-together-agreed-upon-I've-got-company signal. The beacon? The light in the window? *(Beat.)* Burned out? Well, you should've bought some light bulbs before inviting Ellen over. Do you know how embarrassing…how humiliating…how disgusting…to see your roommate in, uh—like that? It's not natural! How would you like to walk in with a pizza, la la la la— and suddenly— *(Makes bed squeaking noise in same stress pattern as la la la la.)* erh-uh-erh-uh! Do you think I could eat after that? And that pizza was my last ten bucks! *(Beat.)* No, I don't want your money—God knows where it's been. *(Beat.)* No, no—there's no way you can make it up to me. *(Beat.)* Tina Summers?! She's lit up every room on the fifth floor! *(Beat.)* You're on.

The Art of Schmoozing

COMEDIC

To his great surprise, Andy, a young actor, runs into Robert DeNiro. He uses the opportunity to try to impress and befriend the film star.

Andy: Oh my God! Oh my frickin' God! You're Robert DeNiro! I can't believe this! It is such an honor to meet you. You are like my hero! I'm serious. *(Imitating DeNiro.)* "You talkin' to me? You talkin' to me?" Not bad, huh? I'm an actor too. Did you see Confessions of a Feminist? I was the guy who got dumped in the very beginning! *(Beat.)* How about The Exterminator? *(Beat.)* No, not The Terminator, The Exterminator. I played the psycho-killer, mutant ant. *(Beat.)* Hey, it's cool. They were nothing compared to your films. *(Accidentally imitating Al Pacino.)* "I'm dyin' over here." *(Beat.)* Huh? Pacino? Oh, yeah, yeah, I knew that — I was, uh, just joking with ya, Bobby. I hear that's what your friends call you — Bobby. Anyway, I've always wanted to ask you this. Are you really in with the mob? *(Silence.)* Ya know what? Don't answer that. It's cool. I'll, uh, see you around.

Award winner: Comedy Monologue Competition, International Modeling & Talent Association, Los Angeles 2000 Convention.

Involuntary Muscles

COMEDIC

Ross has been very stressed out lately. His friend Steve suggested that he take a yoga class. Ross followed his advice, which resulted in an extremely humiliating experience. Ross confronts Steve about what happened.

Ross: I tried, Steve. I really did. I went to a yoga class like you suggested. I thought, you're right, I need to relax. When I walked in, I was the only guy in the whole place. Just me and all of these women! I was thinking, Steve, buddy, you're a genius! Well, the yoga teacher had us all lying down on towels doing this inhale-exhale thing. And suddenly, it became so erotic. I mean, all this heavy breathing and tights. The next thing I know, I got...you know — I couldn't help it! I was mortified! The teacher kept saying, "Feel your body becoming centered." And I'm thinking, all the blood's already rushed to my center! I was struggling — trying to think baseball, calculus, Grandma, but nothing was working! Finally the class ends, everybody leaves, and I'm still lying on the floor! The instructor says she's pleased to see how calm I am. Calm?! I was too humiliated to stand up! Tomorrow, we join kick-boxing.

Award winner: Comedy Monologue Competition, International Modeling & Talent Association, New York 1999 & Los Angeles 2000 Conventions.

Fame and Features

COMEDIC

Ed is a struggling actor who recently decided to try to get an agent. Embittered by the emphasis that was placed on his looks, he played a little joke on the agents with the help of his friend Gary. To his surprise and disgust, it backfired on him.

Ed: Three weeks ago I had auditions for some agents. All on the same day. I go to the first agent, read my copy — she loves it. But she wants me to get my hair cut and dyed. She gives me this salon card and says, "Come back once Pierre fixes you up and then we'll talk." I thought, that's kinda shallow, but hey, I'm willing to change for my craft. I go to the second agent who tells me, "You're very talented, but we've got to do something about your teeth — that space." Look how small this space is! You can barely see it! At this point I'm somewhat disgruntled, but I go to the third agent. He wants me to get a nose job. A nose job! There is nothing wrong with my nose! So today, just for kicks, I ask Gary to go back to these agents with my resume and pretend he's the "new" me. And guess what? He got signed by all three! In my name! They didn't even realize it wasn't me! I'm sickened. As of today, I'm becoming a plumber.

Bench Pressure

COMEDIC

Tony is a personal trainer who works with a variety of clients. After having an awkward and embarrassing experience at a new client's home, Tony tries to get his friend Nick to take over the job.

Tony: Nick, I'm offering you a client who's sixteen. Plus he's got a home gym in his basement. It's easy cash, man. *(Beat.)* Because I'm over there and we're working abs. So I lie down to show him, and the next thing I know his grandma's standing over me, telling him to run to the store for her. And she's wearing this silk robe with all this lacy negligee type stuff. She says I'm doing great working on her grandson, and how about I work on her. Then she drops her robe to the floor! It was a scary friggin' sight! I start to panic and blurt out, "So are you looking to tone-up or get into body building?" Body building?! Everything's sagging to ground-level! She smiles and says, "I was imagining something more…cardiovascular." And I'm thinking, I wonder which one of us would have a heart attack first?! *(Beat.)* Did I what?! She's like 104 years old! You are sick! *(Realizing.)* Nick! This gig is perfect for you!

Award winner: Comedy Monologue Competition, International Modeling & Talent Association, New York 1999 Convention.

The Female Fix

Ron has just been dumped by a girlfriend who insisted on trying to help him change everything she saw in him that wasn't quite right. Still angry and hurt, Ron goes to the GAP to buy a pair of jeans when he is approached by a saleswoman who asks, "Can I help you?" Ron loses it.

Ron: Help me? Can you help me? Did I ask for help? Noooooo. Oh, oh! There's that look! That, that condescending, falsely compassionate, you-need-my-help, let-me-fix-you-since-you're-a-pathetic-guy-and-I'm-the-all-knowing-female look! I am not so pathetic after all. You women are really something. First, you give us guys that sexy, "you want me" look and sucker us in. Then once you've got us hooked, you decide everything that's wrong with us. And then you get this crazy notion that you are the only ones who can help us. Well, Miss GAP, I hate to disappoint you, but I think I'm quite capable of finding a pair of jeans all by myself! I've done it before. I'm a shopper. A shoppee. I'm very, very…shopful. So, if you'll kindly move out of my way…hey! How did you know which kind I—those are my size, but you couldn't have…are you…do you wanna go out sometime?

Feminine Ways

Alan's girlfriend accused him of underestimating the difficulties of being a woman. To appease her, he agreed to "see what it was really like." As a result, Alan has been doing everything his girlfriend asks to understand the female experience. When his girlfriend gives him his latest assignment, Alan decides he has had enough.

Alan: Look, honey, I know you want me to understand what it's like to be you — to be a woman. And haven't I done everything you asked? I watched four movies and counted thirty-seven fat men and only two overweight women. You were right. I sat through sexual harassment workshops and even *volunteered* to be harassed. I shaved my legs to understand what an unfair burden that is. And believe me, that was not easy to explain to the guys at the gym. But this is the limit! I'm sorry, but I am not going to carry around tampons in my briefcase!

The Waiting Womb

Daine got married at a very early age. His wife has been pressuring him to have a baby, and he is not thrilled with the idea. Here, he tells her about a bizarre incident that happened to him today in the hopes that she'll change her mind.

Daine: I know I've been saying that for months, but just hear me out. I'm sitting at a table in the Hilton when I hear, "Excuse me." I look up and this man is standing there with one of those seeing-eye dogs. It totally shocked me. So he says to the wall above my head, "Excuse me, could you tell me how to get to the lobby?" And before I could think I say, "Straight ahead and make a left." Straight ahead and make a left?! Like the guy even knows where straight ahead is. And then I thought, maybe I should have told that to the dog. Suddenly, it hits me: there are two places to turn left. They are doomed! Well, the dog gets to the first opening, looks left, pauses, then turns and leads the man to the lobby! It was amazing! I mean, I actually saw the dog have the thought, "Hmm…directions were left. This *is* the first left. This must be it." Most *people* don't even get that right! And the dog doesn't even speak English! I was floored! So, honey, I really think we should reconsider having a baby, and instead, get ourselves a dog!

MALE MONOLOGUES

DRAMATIC

My Father's Wife

DRAMATIC

After Jason's mother passed away, his father remarried. Jason can't stand his stepmother and resents her for trying to take his mom's place. Today, Jason's teacher, Mr. Beckman, phoned his stepmother to tell her that Jason was causing trouble in class. Jason has just arrived at home when his stepmother confronts him about the phone call.

Jason: Mr. Beckman called you? God, he's so over-the-top. I admit, I was talking in his class. But the real reason he got so mad was because he thought I was talking about him. And I wasn't. He's way too paranoid. So he gave me a detention. It was no big deal. *(Beat.)* Grounded?! What are you talking about? You can't ground me. You're not my mother. Ya know, you have some nerve. You just waltz into the picture and screw with my dad's head until he's so confused and blind that he actually marries you. Oh, I mean, after you threaten him with an ultimatum. *(Beat.)* Bull, you did too. He even told me he didn't really want to marry you, but he was scared of being alone. I told him to get a dog, but no, he didn't listen. So now he's stuck with you. And hey, that was his choice. But not mine. I have a mom. She's dead. But she's still my mom. And nobody will ever take her place. Not you. Not anyone.

Award winner: Drama Monologue Competition, International Modeling & Talent Association, Los Angeles 2000 Convention.

The In Link

DRAMATIC

Aaron is in a special clique — a private computer club with only a few select members. They have set out to use their computer skills to gain programs and inter-net/web access for free, and to have fun. Todd, one of the members, has come up with the club's mission for the day but won't tell Aaron what it is. Curious, Aaron tries to get it out of him.

Aaron: Okay, Todd, what's this cool mission you've got for us? *(Beat.)* A virus? Wait a minute. You want us to spread a new virus? How is that cool? Ya know, when we started our club, we said we wanted to do things that were fun or benefited us. Like all the free months we scammed off AOL. And distorting the pictures on those porn sites. That was fun. Plus, we're up to about $2,000 worth of programs that didn't cost us a penny. But a virus? That serves no purpose but to screw people up. Why would we want to do that to people we don't even know? It isn't entertaining and it doesn't save us money. It goes against our purpose. *(Beat.)* No, I'm not afraid we'll get caught. I'm afraid you're turning into the kind of person we always hated. *(Beat.)* I don't want to get back at them! Or anyone. That's what *you* want, Todd. The only thing I want right now, is out. I quit.

The Back Way Home

DRAMATIC

Bruce is always picking on Trent and making fun of him in front of everyone. Today, as usual, Bruce and his friends have been harassing Trent on his way home from school. Here, Trent finally stands up to him.

Trent: Do it then! You're always threatening to beat the crap out of me. So, come on, Bruce. I'm sure your friends would like to see that. They think you're cool cause you talk like you're so tough. I think you talk that way because you're scared that nobody would like you if you didn't. *(Beat.)* No, I won't shut up! I'm sick of shutting up because you say I should! Every single day of my life I dread walking home because of you. My good times at school are ruined because of you. I have felt like such a loser because you wanted me to. And I let you do that. Well, I'm not gonna let you ruin how I feel anymore. You got that? So either move out of the way once and for all and let me live in peace, or show me what you've really got — right here, right now. Cause I'm not scared of you anymore. So, come on. It's your move.

Role Models

Peter was busted by the cops for smoking pot tonight. Luckily for him, the police were lenient because he is a minor and has no former record. The cops called his mother to come and pick him up at the station. Though fuming inside, his mom didn't say a word to him in the station or the car. When they get home, she explodes, and he is forced to account for his behavior.

Peter: I don't know what I was thinking. I guess I wasn't thinking at all. I mean, I know pot is illegal, but I never imagined I'd wind up in the police station over a couple of dumb joints. *(Beat.)* I realize that now, Mom. Believe me, I will never touch that stuff again. I'm sorry the cops woke you up and you had to come get me. Thanks for not leaving me there. *(Beat.)* What?! How can I not hang out with Tommy? He's my best friend. Mom, it wasn't his fault. *He* didn't bring it. *I* did. *(Beat.)* It doesn't matter where I got it. *(Beat.)* Okay, okay, fine. Bob gave it to me. Your boyfriend, Mom. *(Beat.)* I'm not lying! He's offered it to me a bunch of times before and I said no. He smokes it every day — you know that. You just never want to face it. Ya know, maybe you should have left me at the station. At least someone there might care about what's happening to my life.

The Last to Know

DRAMATIC

Jay's girlfriend has seemed distant the past week or so. It seems as if she is avoiding him. Jay decides to confront her and find out what is going on.

Jay: Can you spare just a minute of your time? I don't think that's too much to ask, considering you're my girlfriend. I know you've been busy with gymnastics and working on the yearbook, but I never get to see you anymore. Vicki told me you went to the movies with her and Michelle last Friday. *We* were supposed to go out, remember? It seems like you're avoiding me or something. You haven't even called me back in five days. Will you please tell me what's going on? I think as your boyfriend I have a right to know. Are you seeing someone else? *(Beat.)* Well…congratulations. That's all I wanted to know. *(Beat.)* Why should you be sorry? It's not like I'm gonna die or anything. It's not like I'm so in love with you, ya know.

In Your Eyes

DRAMATIC

James and Frank are brothers and attend the same high school. School just started back up and Frank is a senior this year. Frank has been ignoring James at school. Now at home, Frank asks James to shoot some hoops, and James finally confronts Frank about the way he's been treating him.

James: Me? You want to shoot some hoops with me? What if someone from school walks by and sees you hanging out with your younger brother? Your life could be ruined instantly. *(Beat.)* What's up with me? No, Frank, "What's up with *you*?" Ever since this semester started you've been totally ignoring me at school. I know you're a big senior this year, but I'm still your brother. What, suddenly you're too cool to be seen with me? I mean, you can't even say hi to me in the hallways? I know I'm only a freshman — big deal! Or am I not popular enough for you? *(Beat.)* don't even say it. You don't have to, I can see it in your eyes. You're so embarrassed to be my brother. Well, don't worry. From now on I don't want to be associated with you either. Not as my brother, not even as my friend.

The Locker Room

Neil hasn't changed for gym class all week. Finally, his teacher sent him to the school counselor. The counselor warns Neil that he is going to fail the class and possibly get suspended if he doesn't start participating again.

Neil: It's only gym class. Who cares. I'm getting A's and B's in everything else. The important stuff. So big deal — "I'm getting an A cause I can throw a ball around." And it's not like I can't do it. I don't like it. I don't like having to...I hate getting changed in the locker room, okay? There are these guys who...they make fun of me all the time. This one guy, Jarred, thinks he's so cool and struts around the locker room naked on purpose. Then he started saying that I was staring at him — like I wanted him or something. And since then, they all call me fag and queer and say I'm gay. They even hid my clothes in the trash and wrote *faggot* across my locker. So I stopped changing for gym. I couldn't tell Mr. Cooper or they would've beat me up. Besides, he likes them cause they're jocks. So he's failing me. You can go ahead and suspend me or give me a million detentions, but I'm not going back in that locker room. Never again.

An Average Guy

DRAMATIC

*Daniel and Sean have been friends for some time now.
Sean is very popular and dates a lot of girls. Daniel is an
average guy who is in love with a girl named Krista.
Sean has just told Daniel that he has a hot date, but is
teasing Daniel by not saying who it is with. Daniel tries
to get him to spill.*

Daniel: Enough already. C'mon, tell me. Who's your big date
with? Erica Dansing? Jenny Larson? *(Beat.)* Okay, I give up.
(Beat.) Krista? Krista Brennon? Jesus, Sean! How could you do
this to me? You know how much I like her. You've never men-
tioned her before. You've been too busy dating all of the most
popular girls in school. Why suddenly Krista? She's the one girl
I really care about. *(Realizing.)* Or is that why you picked her?
To prove to me what a loser I am? Well, guess what Sean?
There's nothing left to prove. I know I'm not as good-looking or
charismatic as you are. You've ingrained that into me over and
over again. You know, the only reason I've stayed friends with
you, is because you made me feel like I'd be nobody without
you. And I believed that. Well, I don't believe it anymore. All
you care about is being popular, no matter how badly you treat
people. I am nothing at all like you. And ya know what? I'm
proud of that.

Award winner: Drama Monologue Competition, International Modeling &
Talent Association, Los Angeles 2000 Convention.

Out of Nowhere

DRAMATIC

Martin and Katie have been going out for a few months. Martin is totally in love with her, and things have been going great. Normally, they meet in the hall during 2nd period, but today Martin couldn't get out of class. After class, he finds her at her locker.

Martin: There you are. Linda told me you were looking for me last period. Mr. Conley wouldn't let me out of class. He said I ask to go to the bathroom so much, I oughta have my bladder checked. I think he's onto us. So did you want to tell me something special or did you just miss me? *(Beat.)* What?! Not see each other anymore? Katie, what are you talking about? Everything's been going great between us. What's happened? *(Beat.)* I don't believe you. A person's feelings can't just change — just disappear — overnight. After all we've been through, everything you said to me, how can you just…Why? I want a reason. *(Beat.)* No, I want a real, concrete reason why. Look me in the eyes and tell me what I've done that's so awful, that you suddenly don't want me in your life anymore.

The Play Back

DRAMATIC

Rob is on the football team at school. Today was the playoffs, and Rob fumbled the ball, causing his team to lose. He feels awful and is hiding out until his teammates leave. His girlfriend, Debbie, finds him, and he decides to confide in her.

Rob: What does it look like I'm doing? I'm hiding till everyone clears out. I can't bear to face them. I don't believe it. I had the ball in my hands. It was a solid catch. And then…I don't know what happened, it just slipped. The last game of the season, the very last play, and I fumbled. Don't you get it? I blew the entire season for everyone. They all hate me now. And I don't blame them. The team worked so hard to make it to the playoffs. We were winning and I…I'm surprised you even want to talk to me. All you're going to hear now is that your boyfriend is a loser. Everyone's going to tell you to dump me. *(Realizing.)* Or is that what you came here to tell me? I mean, what do you want? Do you want me to apologize? Do you want me to make time go backwards? To somehow fix it all?! Huh?! *(Beat.)* Wait! Debbie, wait. I'm sorry. I didn't mean to yell at you. You're the only person I have right now. And I love you. Please stay with me. I'm scared.

In a Dream

Rudy keeps having nightmares about his dad dying. Here, he confronts his father about their underlying meaning.

Rudy: I keep having these dreams, Dad. It's hard to even talk about them. Each one's slightly different, but in every single one of them, you die. It's horrible. I've been scared that it meant something bad was gonna happen to you. I talked to someone about it. She told me that when you kill off — not that I killed you — but when someone dies in your dreams, it usually means that you're killing off their philosophy — their way of life. It clicked. It made sense. And I was so relieved it didn't mean you were going to die. Dad, I don't want to work in the family business. I know how much it means to you. But I can't keep pretending. I'm sorry. I hope somehow you can find a way to be proud of me no matter what career I choose.

A Clean Slate

DRAMATIC

Vince has a history of causing trouble. Since he joined this shop class, the teacher has been like a counselor and mentor, and Vince has cleaned up his act. Today, when an expensive tool is missing, the teacher asks Vince if he stole it. Vince goes off on him because he feels hurt and betrayed.

Vince: So what'dya wanna see me about, Teach? *(Beat.)* Are you kiddin' me? You actually think I stole it?! You're unbelievable, ya know that? After all the time I spent with you this past year…we worked through all that — me and you. What was all that bull about trust between us? Huh? God, you're just as bad as my parents. They never remember the good things, only the bad things I do. And they throw it in my face any time it's convenient. For the rest of my life I'm gonna be the bad one. Even if I grew wings and a halo or saved the world. Why did you bother takin' time to help me straighten up my act? So I'd trust you and believe you were my friend? So I'd think you were proud of me? That maybe there was some good in me? Hell, you shoulda let me go to Juvie. At least I would've known what they really thought of me.

Best Friends

DRAMATIC

Jonathon's girlfriend Kristen admitted that his best friend was trying to get her to sleep with him at a party. Jonathon is shocked because they have been best friends for years. Here, Jonathon confronts his best friend.

Jonathon: "How's it going?" Why don't you tell me? *(Beat.)* Don't even try to pull that "what do you mean?" crap. Kristen told me what you did, so you might as well fess up. *(Beat.)* What do you think she said?! She told me that you were hitting on her and trying to get her real drunk at Rick's party. *(Beat.)* A good time? Exactly what kind of good time did you plan on having with my girlfriend, huh? For Christ's Sake, you're supposed to be my best friend! I mean, after all the shit we've been through together…I trusted you. With my most personal…— everything. It always felt like you were the brother I never had. And suddenly, outta nowhere, you stab me in the back? How could you do that? *(Beat.)* Drunk is not an excuse. If the situation were reversed and I was completely trashed, I admit I might have tried to get some girl to sleep with me. Anyone. Except *your* girl. That's the difference between you and me. I value my friends.

Into the Light

DRAMATIC

Michael and Kathryn have recently become friends, but Kathryn secretly has a crush on him. Kathryn finally musters up the courage to ask him if he wants to go out over the weekend. What she doesn't know is that Michael is gay.

Michael: Friday night? I'm sorry, Kathryn, I already made plans. *(Beat.)* I can't Saturday either. I'm going to, uh, it's just I told a friend of mine we'd go out. *(Beat.)* No, it's not a girl, it's a friend. *(Beat.)* Of course I like you! I think you're wonderful. *(Beat.)* Kathryn, you are not ugly. You're a very attractive girl. It's just...hey, hey, please don't cry. Anyone should consider himself lucky to date someone as incredible as you. I mean it. *(Beat.)* Because I...because...because I'm gay. There, I said it. Please don't look at me like that. It's hard enough feeling like I don't fit in anywhere. Not school, not society, not even with my family. Please don't tell anyone. I'm not ready to deal with being out at school yet. Kathryn? Do you still want to be friends?

Father Figured

DRAMATIC

Brad's father coaches the football team. Today, his father cut one of his best players from the team because he has been slacking due to drugs. Brad's father brought Brad on to take his place, and the player who got cut blames Brad for what happened. Here, Brad refutes that blame.

Brad: It's not my fault you got cut from the team. My dad was doing what he thought was best. If he didn't think I was good enough, he wouldn't have brought me on. He's my dad, I know him. He wouldn't jeopardize the team like that. You're a great player. Everybody knows that. They'd be crazy to say you're not. But you've gotta lay off the drugs. It's hurting your game. I've seen it, and I guess my dad has too. *(Beat.)* Easy! I'm not your enemy, okay? I can't tell you how to live your life. That's your business. But if you really wanna play as bad as you say you do, you gotta make a choice. I'm not stopping you. Neither is my dad. You're stopping yourself.

Award winner: Drama Monologue Competition, International Modeling & Talent Association, Los Angeles 1999 Convention.

Dark Corners

DRAMATIC

Doug's father is an alcoholic. Whenever he drinks, he winds up physically abusing Doug and Doug's mother. Tonight, Doug finally stands up to him.

Doug: Dad, stop it. Just calm down, all right? Take it easy. *(Beat.)* No! No I won't! Stay away from Mom. Do you hear me? I have had it! You wanna go drink yourself to oblivion every night — that's your business. But beating on Mom and slapping me around is over. You got that? *(Beat.)* Look at you. You think you're strong? Does terrorizing your family make you feel powerful, huh? Do you know the principal asked the guys at school who their number one idol was, and 90% of them said their fathers? And all I could think was, I idolize anyone who is nothing at all like my father. Do you realize what an awful feeling that is — as your son — to be ashamed and embarrassed of you? *(Beat.)* I said stay back and I mean it! If you even take one step closer to me and Mom, I swear to God I'll have you thrown in jail for good. You're not the man of this house anymore. Not that you ever were. So either go back to your room and sleep it off, or I call the cops. You choose.

Award winner: Drama Monologue Competition, International Modeling & Talent Association, Los Angeles 2000 Convention.

My Idol, My Enemy

DRAMATIC

Ben's older brother Paul is a straight-A student. Ben studies a lot, but he doesn't get very good grades. Ben both looks up to Paul and envies him. Paul knows that today Ben got the results of his history test and is pestering him to find out how he did. Ben finally tells him.

Ben: I failed my history exam, okay? Are you happy? Now you can tease me as usual and run off to Mom and Dad to brag again. It won't be anything new to them. All I ever hear is, "Paul got straight A's. Paul made the Honor Society. Paul got a scholarship. Why can't you be like him?" Well I can't. I study and study and I try so hard, but I'm not as smart as you. I never will be. Why do you have to rub it in? Don't you realize I've spent my life trying to be as good as you? Trying to keep up. I'm so jealous of you I can't stand it. And all I do is disappoint Mom and Dad all the time. I'm the stupid son — the screw-up, and you're the perfect one. I wish so bad that just once they'd be proud of me. That somehow, some way, they would love me as much as they love you.

Award winner: Drama Monologue Competition, International Modeling & Talent Association, Los Angeles 1999 Convention.

Roses Are Red

DRAMATIC

Craig's mother died of cancer two weeks ago at a very young age. Craig's father has sent him to a therapist to help deal with this tragic loss. Craig does not like the idea of seeing a therapist, but he agrees to go to please his father. Here, he is speaking to the therapist.

Craig: You understand? You understand? No, you *don't* understand. You think just because you have a Ph.D. and a framed certificate on the wall, that you magically know what I'm feeling? What a load of crap. You're just doing your job — making your money. You probably never cared about anyone in your life. Well I do. I care too much. That's why I'm going crazy. I feel like I'm losing my mind. Every time I see a woman who even slightly resembles my mom, I swear she's gonna turn around and it will be her. Alive, here, now, smiling at me. But it never is. I keep waking up in the middle of the night, screaming, all drenched in sweat. Yesterday, I put my fist through the window and shattered it to pieces. My mom is dead. She's dead, and I can't even cry. Cause if I do, it'll mean I accept, really accept, that she's gone forever. I don't want to do that. I *can't* do it. Can you understand that? I can't let my mom be gone.

Family Secrets

Andrew is Lori's older brother. Lori has been dating a guy named Jim. Not knowing where else to turn for help, Lori has just told Andrew that she is pregnant.

Andrew: Jesus Christ. How could you let this happen? Didn't you use protection? Lori, what the hell were you thinking, huh? I mean, that's real bright. Just brilliant. Not to mention that you could get AIDS. How could you not stop to think about that? I'm gonna beat the living crap out of Jim. *(Beat.)* Well, what are ya gonna do — have a baby?! I mean, what, you gonna drop out of school and throw your whole life away?! *(Beat.)* Hey. Hey, I'm sorry. I didn't mean to make you feel worse. It's just, you're my sister, ya know? I feel like I should have been looking out for you more. Then maybe this never woulda happened. *(Beat.)* I know, but…Lori? I want you to know that I'm here for you. I mean it. Whatever you need, come to me. I won't say a word to Mom and Dad. We'll get through this together, okay? Hey. It's gonna be all right. I promise.

Jamming

DRAMATIC

Vic has been playing the drums for five years. He looks up to Warren because Warren is an extremely talented musician and his band is doing very well. When Vic hears that Warren's drummer quit the band, he tries to persuade Warren to give him a shot as their new drummer.

Vic: Hey, Warren. I heard Chuck quit on you. That sucks, man. He's a really good drummer. I've seen you play over a dozen times. You guys were hot. You blow Reactive Souls away. He's crazy to bail on you for them. What are you planning on doing? *(Beat.)* How about me? I've been playing drums for about five years now. I've got a bitchin' 10-piece Ludwig set, plus a back-up 7-piece Tama kit. *(Beat.)* I know my style's a little different, but I'm ready for a change. Besides, I've seen you play so many times, I practically know all your tunes. Look, all I'm asking is that you give me a shot. You guys have so much potential — you're tight, you're dedicated, and you've got a decent following. I'd hate to see you throw it all away. Let me jam with you — just one time, that's it. Then you decide. Whadda you say?

Gettin' Out

Louis has had a hard life. He grew up in a very danger-ous neighborhood. Recently, he landed a football schol-arship at a prestigious college. It is the first day of prac-tice, and his coach has been busting Louis' butt, trying to see if he has what it takes or wants to run home to Mama. Louis sets him straight.

Louis: Look coach, I know it's your job to try to scare the living crap out of us the first day of practice. And I don't mean you no disrespect, but you can save your breath with me. I've spent my life hearing gunshots. Watching ten-year-old kids roaming the streets for a fix. Seeing my friends' bodies being taken away in ambulances. Trying to get from the bus to my house without getting a knife held to my throat or stuck in my back. So, no offense coach, but knocking heads or bustin' a knee cap ain't about to scare me. I'm not like those rich kids who are here so they can brag about their free ride. This scholarship is my tick-et out of a life headed for dealing drugs or an early coffin. And not one moment will go by that I don't say my thanks to God and to you for giving me this opportunity. You didn't make a mistake bringing me on, coach. I'll make you proud. Just watch. You'll see.

The Reflection

Scott and Dawn have been dating. Dawn has been burned before and is scared of getting hurt again. As a result, she continually starts fights and tries to test Scott — to push him away. Scott truly loves Dawn and understands why she acts the way she does. Here, Dawn has just accused Scott of not really caring about her, and he retorts.

Scott: Okay, you're right! I lied about everything. I *don't* really like you. I think you're selfish and boring and ugly. I was just using you and now it's time to say, "See ya. Thanks for a lame time!" Is that want you want to hear? Huh? Does that make you feel better? Jesus, Dawn, if you could only see yourself through my eyes, you'd know how special and wonderful you are. I've never met a more passionate, fragile, stubborn, honest, feisty, beautiful person in my life. I love you. And if you don't love yourself right now — okay, I accept that. But please, let *me* love you. Don't push me away. I don't want to be with anyone else. Just you, Dawn. You.

Award winner: Drama Monologue Competition, International Modeling & Talent Association, Los Angeles 2000 Convention.

In the Name of Fame

DRAMATIC

After years of hard work, Johnny's band finally landed a big tour. The only problem is that Johnny's guitarist has been blowing off rehearsals and partying too much. Johnny and the other band members had a serious discussion and decided to replace him. Johnny has the unpleasant job of breaking the news to him.

Johnny: I said you're out, man, and I mean it. You ain't got no dedication. Half the time you don't even show up for rehearsal, and the other half you're late or drunk. This ain't no puberty garage band no more. We've finally got our big break with this tour, and hell if I'm gonna let you screw it up. I've worked too hard for this — so have the guys. You want the fame and money handed to you on a silver platter while you sit back on your lazy ass getting trashed. It don't work that way. You gotta earn it. We ain't givin' you a free ride. You had plenty of warnings and you ignored them all. Look, you're a hot guitarist. Nobody's questioning your talent. But that ain't enough in this business. I'm real sorry, man. It's final. The tour is going on, but you're not.

Black and Blue

Pete has had a tough life. He's been through a lot of hard times and learned not to rely on anyone but himself. He's been dating a woman and to his surprise has fallen in love with her. Terrified, he decides to break it off, though deep down he really wants to be with her.

Pete: Whoa. My lips are moving, I'm making sound. I know I ain't talking no foreign language. So why is it you don't hear what I'm saying? I don't want to be with you no more. It ain't a difficult sentence to understand. *(Beat.)* Yeah, yeah, I know — I'm mean, cruel — *(Beat.).* Heartless? No, no, that's exactly what I'm trying *not* to be. I got a heart inside of me. It's this small, little organ thing. But that little thing has got some awful big feelings. I ain't never been scared of nothing in my life and I've had my share of bad things happen. But they heal up — just some scars left, see? But your *heart*, if that gets stomped on, gets broken, you die. Period. And you got my heart right there in your hands. And I got an uneasy feeling cause you could do the smallest thing and it would break right in half. Just like that. And I ain't ready to be dying. I don't wanna know what that feels like.

Award winner: Drama Monologue Competition, International Modeling & Talent Association, Los Angeles 1999 Convention.

In the Blood

DRAMATIC

Mike and John are brothers. They just received a phone call from their sister. She is a cocaine addict and has gotten herself into big trouble. She desperately needs their help. John does not want to go. Mike, on the other hand, immediately drops everything and is ready to fly out to see her.

Mike: I don't care what she did. It doesn't matter. She's our sister, John. Who's gonna help her if we don't? Nobody, that's who. *(Beat.)* So cocaine is illegal — I know. But she didn't get into it herself, did she? Somebody turned her onto it and she's been struggling with it ever since. Ever think about what your drinking did to her? No, why would you? Alcohol is legal — it's not coke. What crap! Drugs are drugs — addiction is addiction. She learned from you how to numb out and you can't even lift a finger to help her. Cause you're sober now — life is good. You're so selfish it makes me sick. Well, I'm going. I'm sure you can run the business just fine while I'm gone. In fact, why don't you find yourself a new partner. Family can be so unreliable.

MALE or FEMALE MONOLOGUES

COMEDIC

The Last Meal

M OR F, COMEDIC

After being caught in the middle of a food fight on the last day of school, Jamie defends himself/herself to the school disciplinarian.

Jamie: It's the last day of school! What's the big deal? Nobody eats it anyway. It's cafeteria food, it's not like it's Burger King. Besides, it happened in third period and fourth period and nobody got in trouble then! I didn't even start it — it was self-defense! Somebody smacked me in the eye with a hot dog — I had to retaliate. I only rifled three Tator Tots. That's it! And two of them missed! But Gordan went ahead and waled me anyway, with a big bran muffin. With nuts! Right in the neck! See the welt? I almost choked! I could sue the school for millions! Not to mention malnutrition. *(Beat.)* In-school suspension? You've got to be kidding. *(Beat.)* Do I get lunch with that?

Eating Up Profits

M OR F, COMEDIC

Jerri works in Mr. Reilly's bakery. Mr. Reilly just caught Jerri pigging out on the baked goods. Here, Jerri attempts to convince Mr. Reilly that he/she was sampling the desserts for the sake of the business.

Jerri: Okay, I know I ate some cheesecake and a double chocolate peanut butter cookie and a lemon tart. But I can explain that, Mr. Reilly. You see, customers come into your bakery every day. And no matter what they're considering buying, they ask me if it's good. And when I say yes — like you told me to — they still always ask, "Have you tried it?" Now I could lie and say yes, but it goes against my nature. Plus, I'm a terrible liar. But when I say no, they have second thoughts. Sometimes they leave right away — walk out without buying anything. And that's awful for business. So I figured, if I taste one of everything then I could really say yes! Don't you see? I'm not eating up your profits, I'm increasing them! *(Beat.)* Fired?! You've got to be kidding? That's the thanks I get for helping your business. Fine. Oh, by the way? Your lemon tarts suck!

Award winner: Comedy Monologue Competition, International Modeling & Talent Association, Los Angeles 2000 Convention.

Writing Out Loud

M OR F, COMEDIC

Pat has recently been studying and experimenting with poetry. As with many new writers, Pat is excited, motivated, and a bit naive. Pat decides to ask a friend and mentor, who is a published poet, for advice on his/her latest poem.

Pat: Yes, of course I want you to be honest, but how can you not like it? It's a good poem. Don't you get the images, the analogies, the use of onomatopoeia? I mean, I asked for your opinion because you're a seasoned poet and you say what you feel. But there's nothing not to like! Don't you agree? Here — look at this line, "Like chimney-chestnut-roasted tea." That's so specific you can smell it — taste it. Right? Right? Am I right? *(Beat.)* Ohhhh, I see. You're jealous. That's it, isn't it? Your jealous because I don't have writers' block. Because my work is fresh, inspired, avant-garde, and you're still scrawling out that old sappy sonnet style stuff. Did you hear that? I'm even speaking with alliteration! Thanks for the feedback. I feel so much better!

Award winner: Comedy Monologue Competition, International Modeling & Talent Association, Los Angeles 1999 Convention.

MALE or FEMALE MONOLOGUES

DRAMATIC

Einstein's Best Friend

M OR F, DRAMATIC

Lee and Dean are best friends. Lee has always admired and envied Dean because he is so smart. Dean has just won 1st Runner-up at the state science fair. Lee is thrilled; Dean is not.

Lee: Congratulations, Mr. First Runner-up of the state science fair! Can I have your autograph now, before you're building missiles or saving the world? *(Beat.)* What's wrong? *(Beat.)* Wait a minute — whoa. Are you telling me that you're bummed because you didn't get first place? My God Dean, you've got to be kidding me. Do you realize how many contestants there were? That what you achieved is incredible?! Ya know, you're my best friend, but I have to tell you that you are the most selfish, conceited idiot I've ever known. All you can see is what you don't have — the little tiny things — instead of realizing how many gifts you do have. There are thousands of people who would kill to be in your shoes. *I* would kill to be in your shoes. I'd give anything to have just one of your talents. To be noticed and honored. To feel special. Just once. Ya know Dean, you're so smart, that you can't even see how stupid you are.

Award winner: Drama Monologue Competition, International Modeling & Talent Association, Los Angeles 2000 Convention.

The Big Move

M OR F, DRAMATIC

Drew and his/her girlfriend/boyfriend have been anxiously awaiting the news of which colleges accepted them. They have planned to go to the same college. Drew just found out that he/she was accepted to Purdue and is very excited. Drew's girlfriend/boyfriend was accepted to NYU.

Drew: Okay, okay, okay. I got accepted to Purdue! Dun-da-da-dah! I'm so psyched — I can't believe it! I know you'll get in no problem. Have you heard from them yet? *(Beat.)* NYU? Wow, no kidding? That's fabulous. The Big Apple, huh? That's…that's really great. Are you gonna go? *(Beat.)* I know, I know — it's a great opportunity for you, it's just…I thought we were gonna be together. I mean, that was the plan, remember? You told me that no matter what happens, you wanted to be with me. So, what, did you suddenly change your mind? You just wanna break up now? *(Beat.)* Writing is not the same. Four years is a long time. You'll make new friends, meet new…people. I don't want to lose you. You know what? Forget Purdue. I'll move to New York with you. I'll get a job and apply to NYU next year. *(Beat.)* Hey, hey, shhh. I want to. Don't you get it? I can't picture my life without you.

Look Upon Me

M OR F, DRAMATIC

Brooke is an actor. Brooke was playing a game with his/her family and his/her dad had to get his team to guess "Hamlet." As his clue, Brooke's father said, "Brooke did this play." Brooke was never in "Hamlet." Upset that his/her father didn't even know which plays Brooke had done, Brooke stormed out of the room. Brooke's dad followed to see why Brooke got so upset.

Brooke: It wasn't the stupid game. I don't care about that. It was your clue for *Hamlet*. You said, "Brooke did this play." I never did *Hamlet*, Dad, I did *King Lear*. But you didn't know that because you've never come to see any of my shows since the beginning of high school. Mom and Gail have been to all of them. All of them! Even when I was performing out in Kentucky and Milwaukee. I know you're busy with work, but if it was important to you, you would have come to at least one. I'm sorry I turned down Law School, okay? But I'm not you, Dad. I'm an actor. That's what I want to do with my life. *King Lear* was my biggest accomplishment. And when you didn't show up, I was so hurt because I felt like you didn't care. Why can't you be proud of me, Dad? That's all I want. Please come to my next show. Let me know that it matters to you.

Gemini Rising

M OR F, DRAMATIC

Tori has big dreams of becoming famous. However, due to fear, Tori has not been actively pursuing his/her dream for over two years now. Tori turns to a good friend for advice.

Tori: I'm not in a slump. A slump is short. It's been two-and-a-half years now. It's the duality thing. Haven't you ever felt that? To like someone and be disgusted by them at the same time. To want your goals and be afraid of getting them. To know deep inside that you're good, you're talented, you can do it. While the other half of you says, "Who are you kidding? You suck. You'll never get there." And the thing is, it can switch on me like that. *(Snaps.)* I never know which side will take over at any moment. It's awful. It makes me get stuck — I can't do anything. But I know I've gotta move. Because if I stay frozen like this, my dream will fade away and it'll be too late. It's not like making a decision. I can't seem to kill off my passion, or the fear of failing. What am I supposed to do?

THE AUTHOR

Janet B. Milstein is an actress, acting teacher, and private monologue coach. She received her MFA in Acting from Binghamton University in New York, and her BA in Theatre with Distinction from the University of Delaware. Janet has an extensive background in theatre, having worked with numerous theatres and companies, including the Milwaukee Repertory Theater, the Pabst Theater, the Organic Theater, the Theatre Building, the Athenaeum Studio Theatre, National Pastime Theater, Stage Left Theatre, Mary-Arrchie Theatre Co., the Women's Theatre Alliance, Theatre Q, Chicago Dramatists, Tinfish Productions, Cafe Voltaire, and more. Janet has appeared in several independent films, as well as working in industrials and voice-overs.

Janet has taught acting to undergraduates at Binghamton University, to apprentices at Fort Harrod Drama Productions, and to children and adults at various acting workshops. Since 1997, she has been teaching acting at John Robert Powers Entertainment Company, Chicago, where she was named Best Instructor. In addition to teaching many levels of acting classes at John Robert Powers, Janet trains talent contestants for competition at the bi-annual International Modeling and Talent Association conventions in New York and Los Angeles.

Janet also works as a private acting coach in Chicago. She trains beginners and professional actors in monologues and cold readings. If you would like to contact the author, you can e-mail her at Monolog123@aol.com.